Bruckner

Anton Bruckner. Bust by Franz S. Forster

Bruckner

HANS-HUBERT SCHÖNZELER

GROSSMAN PUBLISHERS, NEW YORK 1970

Published by Grossman Publishers, Inc.
125A East 19th Street, New York, N.Y. 10003

Library of Congress Catalogue Card Number: 78-114931

Manufactured in Great Britain
First Printing

Bruckner

by

HANS-HUBERT SCHÖNZELER

Contents

His Life

In any review of the growth and development of music in the late eighteenth and the nineteenth centuries, Austria and particularly Vienna stand out as occupying a dominant position, and indeed the list of composers who lived and worked there during that period includes a large number of names which have since become household words. Yet it is strange that of this imposing array of great musicians comparatively few are of entirely Austrian origin. Many of them are from the surrounding countries, especially Bohemia and Hungary. Beethoven and Brahms, for instance, can lay no claim whatever to Austrian heritage, merely having chosen Vienna as their home, and amongst the great ones only Schubert and Johann Strauss can truly be called Viennese. Strangest of all, Mozart, the musical personification of Austria, is of Austrian descent on his mother's side only, his father Leopold Mozart having been born in Augsburg of an old German family.

Anton Bruckner, however, was Austrian to the very core. Through detailed and meticulous research Ernst Schwanzara has traced Bruckner's ancestry back to the beginning of the fifteenth century and has proved that throughout the five ensuing centuries the Bruckners have always lived in the proximity of Linz.[1] The first forebear of Anton Bruckner for whom authentic documentation could be found was Jörg Prukner, born in about 1400, a peasant under the then prevalent feudal system. His holding was in the vicinity of Oed, some twenty-five miles east of Linz, and it would appear that both house and family took their name from the fact that the homestead was situated near a bridge (German *Brücke*, with its old Austrian form *Pruck*) over a small stream. There the family continued as peasants and farmers, generation after generation, until we come to Anton Bruckner's great-grandfather, Josef Bruckner, born 1715 in Pyhra near Oed. Acquiring some wealth by his marriage, he left the ancestral home

[1] Göllerich-Auer, *Anton Bruckner*, Regensburg, 1922–1936

The Brucknerhof (*Pyhra near Oed*) *as it stands today*

and settled in Oed as a house-owner, innkeeper and broom-maker.[1] One of his sons, also named Josef, at first continued in his father's footsteps as a broom-maker, but following an inner urge he soon turned to the teaching profession. In Linz he took the prescribed course for assistant teachers (which in those days took all of six weeks!), and after working as a teacher in various places for some ten years, he was finally posted to Ansfelden near Linz in Upper Austria in 1776—forty-eight years before his grandson was to be born in that same Ansfelden. Josef Bruckner had twelve children, and one of them, Anton, born in 1791, became a teacher like his father. Initially he acted as his father's assistant and after his father's retirement became his successor. In 1823 he married Therese Helm from Steyr, a marriage which was to be blessed with eleven children, of whom only five lived to reach the age of maturity. Their eldest was Josef Anton, born on 4 September 1824 and named after his father and grandfather—the Bruckner who was to make the family name resound throughout the world.

Such is the ancestry and such are the relatively humble beginnings of the man who was to become one of the greatest symphonists this world has known. Nor was his life particularly eventful. The life stories of many of the great composers combine a wealth of variety with a sequence of events which might well stem from some novelist's fertile imagination, but Anton Bruckner's life is entirely devoid of such picturesque and spectacular traits. His was a life of

[1] In consequence of Josef Bruckner's move to Oed, the homestead went to his sister who was married to a man named Hagler. From that time up to the present day the '*Brucknerhof*' has been in the possession of the Hagler family.

Bruckner's birthplace, Ansfelden. Bruckner was born in the ground-floor room at this corner

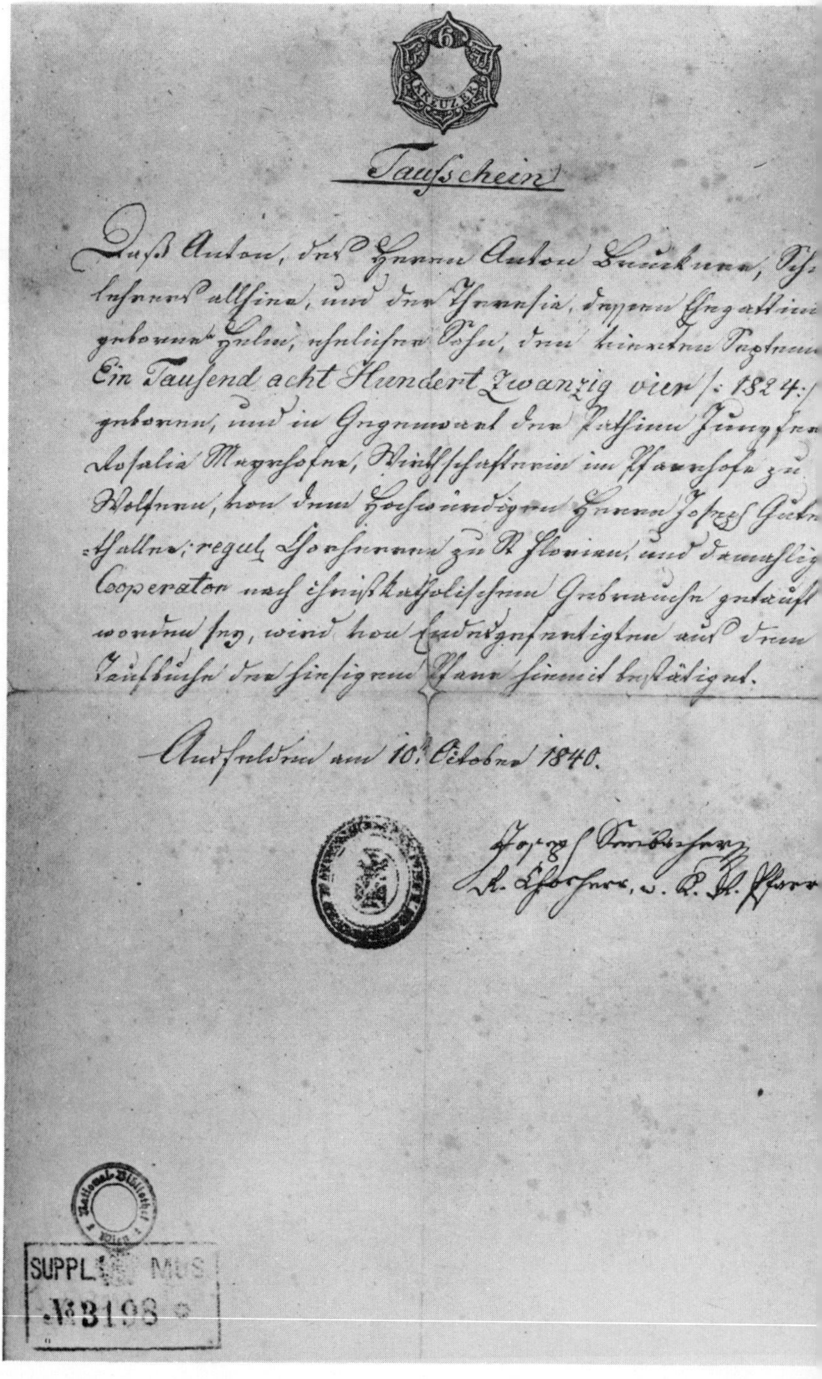

Taufschein

Daß Anton, des Herrn Anton Bruckner, Schullehrers allhier, und der Theresia, dessen Ehegattin geborne Helm, ehelicher Sohn, den vierten September Ein Tausend acht Hundert Zwanzig vier /: 1824 :/ geboren, und in Gegenwart der Pathinn Jungfrau Rosalia Mayrhofer, Wirthschafterinn im Pfarrhofe zu Wolfern, von dem Hochwürdigen Herrn Joseph [illegible] regul. Chorherrn zu St. Florian, und damaligen Cooperator nach christkatholischem Gebrauche getauft worden sey, wird vom Endesgefertigten aus dem Taufbuche der hiesigen Pfarr hiermit bestätiget.

Ansfelden am 10. October 1840.

Joseph [illegible]
reg. Chorherr, d. P. [illegible] Pfarrer

Ihrem Ehrenmitgliede
dem berühmten Tondichter
Dr. ANTON BRUCKNER
Ritter des Franz Joseph Ordens
k.k. Hoforganist, Lector an der
k.k. Universität in Wien
Ehrenbürger der Landeshauptstadt
Linz
geb. in diesem Hause, am 4. Sept. 1824
widmet diese Gedenktafel
die Liedertafel Frohsinn in Linz
Mai 1895

Memorial plaque on the house in which Bruckner was born

Bruckner's certificate of baptism

Ansfelden, the village church with the house in which Bruckner was born

St. Florian, west façade

Hörsching church

severity, at times of hardships, struggles and disappointments, a life completely devoted to a single cause: his music. He travelled little, and what few journeys he did undertake were for the most part undertaken for professional reasons and in the interests of his music. In short, the story of Bruckner's life is virtually synonymous with the story of the growth of his music.

The three children born after 'Tonerl', as the little Anton was called at home, all died in infancy, and so it is not surprising that the parents lavished on their first-born all their sheltering parental love. Nevertheless Anton grew up as a normal boy, with no hint of precocity, and on more than one occasion

Stift St. Florian

his pranks seem to have landed him in trouble. But right from the start music played an important part in his life, for his mother, who had a beautiful voice and sang in the church choir, took him with her to High Mass from his earliest childhood. In church Tonerl's favourite place was on the organ bench by his father's side.[1]

At the age of four he was already playing some of the church hymns on his child's violin, and soon afterwards he made his first attempts at playing his

[1] In those days in Austria, the village schoolmaster was usually the church organist as well.

St. Florian, the Great Staircase

father's old spinet. Father Bruckner, himself an ardent musician, was quick to notice his eldest son's interest and talent and encouraged it in every possible way, so that by the time young Anton was ten he was deputising for his father on the organ bench. The church of Ansfelden also boasted an 'orchestra' consisting of two violins, double bass, clarinet and horn, and on special occasions two trumpeters and a timpanist were engaged from Linz. Days such as these were musical feasts for the boy who gloried in the sound of the trumpets, and it is quite conceivable that here, in the village church of Ansfelden, the foundation was laid for that magnificently rich brass sound which marks the climax of almost every one of Bruckner's later works. It must have been at this time, when Anton was about ten, that his parents began to take him on occasional visits to the Stift St. Florian[1] which was to become his spiritual home for the rest of his life. There he heard the great organ, now known as the 'Bruckner Organ', which he was to play so often and beneath which, eventually, he was to find his last resting place. The sound of this splendid instrument must have made an enormous impression on the receptive mind of the young boy who up until then had only known the relatively modest organ of the Ansfelden church.

The year 1835 marks the first change in the course of Anton Bruckner's life. He was now eleven, and meanwhile the family in the schoolmaster's house

[1] In the case of St. Florian the word *Stift* denotes a community of ordained priests living together as an Augustinian monastic order.

St. Florian, Prandtauer Gate

Windhaag

had increased by four more children: Rosalie, Josefa, Maria Anna ('Nani') and Ignaz. As the house was becoming somewhat cramped for this large family, Anton was sent to his godfather, Johann Baptist Weiss, schoolteacher and organist in Hörsching near Linz, and with him he spent the best part of two years, from the spring of 1835 until December 1836. Under the direction of his godfather Anton Bruckner received his first regular tuition on the organ as well as in the theory of music, with special emphasis on the art of playing the organ from a figured bass. Hörsching also commanded much better musical facilities than Ansfelden, which gave Anton the opportunity of hearing such works as Haydn's *Creation* and *The Seasons* as well as Mozart's Masses, and thereby his musical horizon was widened considerably. It was probably also during this period that Bruckner made his first attempts at organ improvisation, a field in which he was later to become an uncontested master. In these improvisations he went far beyond the few small-scale organ compositions which date from that time.[1] The years in Hörsching were happy years for the boy,

[1] Max Auer inclines to the opinion that the *Pange lingua* in C for mixed chorus also dates from the Hörsching years, whereas Robert Haas ascribes it to the Windhaag period, 1841–43. See Max Auer, *Anton Bruckner*, Vienna, 1932; and Robert Haas, *Anton Bruckner*, Potsdam, 1934.

The old school house, Windhaag

and it is to Weiss's credit that despite Anton's obvious musical talent he did not neglect his general education.

Foreshadowing the pattern that was to characterise Bruckner's entire life, these two happiest years of his childhood were to be followed by years of deepest grief. Bruckner's father fell fatally ill in December 1836, and Anton was immediately called back to Ansfelden. At home matters were in a distressing state. In order to support his large family the father had been compelled to augment his income by playing the fiddle at village dances, often until late at night, and as his duties commenced with ringing the church bells at four or five o'clock in the morning, his strength had rapidly and prematurely deteriorated. Now it was up to Anton as the eldest son, a mere boy of twelve, to step into the breach and deputise for the father whenever the need arose—in school, in church or as fiddler on the dance floor. Anton had often had to accompany the priest when visiting the dying, so that from his earliest youth Death was a familiar figure to him, but never had he felt its grimness as acutely as on the day when the priest gave Extreme Unction to his father, and when he saw his father die on 7 June 1837.

Although Bruckner's mother was given to fits of depression, a trait which Bruckner seems to have inherited from her and which will be mentioned again when we discuss his character, her resolute manner asserted itself in times of crisis, and on the very day of her husband's death she took Anton to the Stift St. Florian to ask the prior Michael Arneth to accept him as a choir boy. Despite the fact that Anton's beautiful soprano voice was near to breaking, Arneth granted the mother's wish, and until his death in 1854 he remained Bruckner's staunch friend and helper. Thus in 1836 St. Florian became Bruckner's home, while his mother, with the remaining four children, moved to Ebelsberg where she eked out a living until her death there in 1860.

St. Florian plays such an important part in Bruckner's life that a few words at least must be said about it. Situated about ten miles to the south-east of Linz it marks the spot where, according to legend, the body of the Roman Florianus was buried after he had suffered a martyr's death. A monastery on the site is first mentioned in documents dating back to about 800, and from 1071 it was an Augustinian *Chorherrenstift*. From then onwards its history runs parallel to that of many similar institutions and is dominated by political events, by the Reformation and the wars against the Turks, but the great turning-point came towards the end of the seventeenth century when its financial position had become secure. Under the prelate David Fuhrmann an ambitious building programme was put into execution, and during the years 1686–1751 the Stift

Franz Josef Rudigier, Bishop of Linz (died 1884)

St. Florian as it stands to-day came into being. Designed by the Milanese architect Carlo Carlone, the building was begun under his supervision. After Carlone's death it was continued in accordance with his plans by the well-known Austrian architect Jakob Prandtauer, and after him by Jakob Steinhuber. As a whole St. Florian is perhaps one of the most glorious manifestations of baroque architecture. Designed to fit into its natural surroundings, the entire complex is absolutely perfect in its proportions and of such a generous spaciousness that despite its tremendous size it never gives the visitor any feeling of oppressiveness.

Such, then, was the place which can truly be called Bruckner's spiritual home. It was also his actual home during the periods 1837–40 and 1845–55, and in later life, when Bruckner was living in Linz and Vienna, he spent many of his holidays at St. Florian, often retreating there when the burden which fate had placed on his shoulders seemed too heavy to bear. For this reason St. Florian will always find a prominent place in every Bruckner biography, but perhaps it has not been sufficiently stressed that in fact it represents the very essence of Bruckner and reflects virtually every facet of his musical output: the glory of its baroque architecture, cradled in the gentle hillside of the Upper Austrian landscape, the fervour of its cloistered and mystical catholicism, the sound of the great organ in the *Stiftskirche*, the *memento mori* atmosphere of its dark and narrow catacombs and crypts—these are the elements which formed and conditioned the receptive mind of the boy and which are the basis for the symphonic utterances of the mature man.

In St. Florian the thirteen-year-old boy continued his schooling, and together with the other two choirboys he lodged with the family of the headmaster, Bogner. In St. Florian's school he was taught reading, writing and arithmetic, and his education also embraced lessons on the organ, the violin and in musical theory. But it was the organ in particular which attracted Tonerl, and when at the age of fourteen he had completed his official schooling it was to the organ and especially to free improvisation on the organ that he devoted most of his time. In this latter field he found a great example in the organist of St. Florian, Anton Kattinger, referred to by many of his contempories as 'the Beethoven of the organ'. When Anton Bruckner reached the age of fifteen his voice began to break and he had to be replaced in the choir. However, he still fulfilled his part in the musical life of St. Florian as a violinist, and occasionally he was also allowed to play the organ for the minor religious services.

But the boy was growing up, and plans had to be made for his future. One day Michael Arneth, who had become very fond of young Bruckner, took him aside and asked: 'Well, Tonerl, what would you like to be: a priest, a schoolteacher, or perhaps you would like to study?' Without hesitation Anton replied: 'A teacher, like my father.' It is reputed that in later years Bruckner commented on that decision, saying that it was made out of a feeling of filial piety, but it is also very likely that his choice was influenced by the fact that in the teaching profession he knew he would soon be in a position to give at least some small financial assistance to his mother and his brother and sisters. However this may be, the kindly prelate granted Bruckner's wish. Accordingly

Tonerl was coached for the *Präparandie*, as the training school for aspiring teachers was called, and in October 1840 he passed the entrance examination in Linz.

The year in Linz (1840–41) constitutes the beginning of a new section in Bruckner's life; one might almost call it the beginning of his manhood. It must have been bewildering for him, having grown up in the village atmosphere of Ansfelden and Hörsching and in the monastic calm of St. Florian, to find himself suddenly transplanted into the hustle and bustle of the capital of Upper Austria. Although Bruckner was to spend the greater part of his subsequent life (forty-one years, to be exact) in the towns of Linz and Vienna, he never became a 'city-dweller' in the real sense of the term. It is presumably this facet of Bruckner's character that has prompted some biographers to exaggerated accounts of his 'peasant nature'.

At the *Präparandie* Bruckner proved a model student, and at the end of the ten months' course he passed the final examination with flying colours—an unusual occurrence, for as a rule the majority of students had to repeat the year. But far more important are the musical contacts which Bruckner made during that time. As the village schoolmaster in those days also had to supply the music in the village church, all musical subjects were of prime importance in this training course. These were taught by August Dürrnberger who was also the author of a book on musical theory. A close personal friendship soon sprang up between Bruckner and Dürrnberger, and in later years, when Bruckner himself had become a professor of musical theory in Vienna, he said that he owed everything to Dürrnberger's book and consistently used it as a basis for his teaching. In Linz Bruckner also had the opportunity of hearing more music than ever before. Although the theatre, considered a 'hotbed of dissipation', was out of bounds to pupils of the *Präparandie*, in church Bruckner became more and more familiar with the sacred music of the Viennese classics, in particular with the Masses of Haydn and Mozart, and in the concerts of the Music Association he first came in contact with the secular music of his day, such as Weber's Overtures and especially Beethoven's Symphonies, from which he received an entirely new stimulus.

All too quickly the year passed by, and in August 1841 Bruckner found himself the possessor of a certificate proclaiming him an 'assistant teacher for elementary schools'. In due course he received his first appointment, as assistant teacher in the small village of Windhaag near the Bohemian border, but before proceeding there he spent a few weeks in St. Florian and possibly also some time with his mother in Ebelsberg. It must have been a day of pride and joy for his mother to see her eldest son, for whom she had sacrificed so much, ready to take up his chosen profession. For Bruckner himself it must have been a source of great satisfaction that he would now be able to give, albeit on a very modest scale, where up to now he had been compelled only to receive. Far too little mention has been made of the way in which, throughout his life, Bruckner cared for those nearest and dearest to him, financially as well as humanly, and two letters bear eloquent witness to this fact. The first of these, written to

Plaque on the old school house, Windhaag

Bruckner by his sister Rosalie shortly after his seventieth birthday, contains the following passage:

> 'We have read so much about you in the newspapers, but one important thing they have all forgotten to mention: how wonderfully you have always supported your dear departed mother and your brother and sisters with the money which you have had to earn with so much hard toil.'

One of Bruckner's very last letters to his brother Ignaz in St. Florian reads as follows:

> 'My dear little Brother! All the very best for the new year. Ignaz, look after your money! We Bruckners aren't so rich that we can afford to lend our money. Anton.'

View of Kronstorf

Bruckner stayed in Windhaag for fifteen months, from October 1841 until January 1843, and in the main it was a period of base servitude. The village at that time numbered about 35 houses and 200 inhabitants, and by all accounts he appears to have been well-liked by the villagers. The assistant teacher, however, was completely subject to the will and whims of his superior. In Bruckner's case, he had not only to fulfil his duties in school and in church; he also had to fetch and carry for the teacher and work in his fields after school. He even had to spread manure, and take his meals with the servant girl. Altogether he felt very much like an exile in Windhaag and sought consolation in his belief in God and in his beloved music. In the church he had an organ at his disposal, and to further his theoretical knowledge he studied Bach's *Art of the Fugue* and the fugues of Albrechtsberger. During the months in Windhaag he also tried his hand at composition with a small-scale Mass in C for solo alto, organ and two horns. His only relaxation and enjoyment during this time was

The former school house, Kronstorf. Bruckner lived in the first floor rooms, the windows of which are on either side of the memorial plaque

Main nave of the Stadtpfarrkirche, *Steyr*

the dance-floor where, like his father, he played the violin to augment his sparse salary. It is said that on numerous occasions Bruckner improvised dance melodies on his violin, and it is conceivable that in some of the scherzi of his later symphonies he harked back to those days. The schoolmaster Fuchs, however, viewed the musical ambitions of his assistant with ever-growing displeasure, and when Arneth came to Windhaag on a tour of inspection Fuchs took the opportunity of complaining bitterly about Bruckner. Arneth took in the situation immediately, and as there was no vacancy at St. Florian he found a position in Kronstorf for Bruckner until such time as he should be able to return to St. Florian.

Kronstorf was even smaller than Windhaag, numbering only about 100 inhabitants in those days, yet Bruckner found much more happiness there, and until late in life he looked back on his Kronstorf days (from January 1843 to September 1845) with evident pleasure. The village is situated about half-way between Enns and Steyr, only two and a half hours' walk from St. Florian, and here he was again in the familiar and beloved landscape of his childhood and youth. Although he still fulfilled the subservient role of assistant teacher with all the duties that went with this position, he found a true home with the schoolmaster, Franz S. Lehofer, whose wife looked after Bruckner's needs like a mother; he remembered her with affection and gratitude even in his old age. In addition his salary, initially the same as in Windhaag (12 guilders *per annum*), was soon increased to 20 guilders, which enabled him to help his mother and the other children more effectively.

The most important aspect of these years in Kronstorf, however, and that which is of more particular interest to us, is the musical one. In Kronstorf itself Bruckner soon found new friends and there was much music-making, especially with the farmer Josef Födermayer through whose generosity he had a spinet at his disposal in his schoolroom. Frequent visits to St. Florian also provided a musical stimulus. Most important, however, was the proximity of the two towns of Enns and Steyr. In Enns Bruckner made friends with the choirmaster, Leopold von Zenetti, whom he already knew from his days in St. Florian, and Zenetti undertook the further theoretical education of the young man. Apart from the textbook by D. G. Türk, Zenetti based his teaching in the main on Bach's chorales and the *Welltempered Clavier*, thereby laying one of the most important foundation-stones of Bruckner's later work. Three times every week the pupil Anton made his way to his revered teacher in Enns to receive instruction and submit his 'homework'. In Steyr Bruckner was to find another home from home in the presbytery of the Steyr priest Joseph Plersch to whom the priest in Windhaag had given him an introduction, and like St. Florian, Steyr remained a place of refuge and retreat for the rest of his life. St. Florian had imbued the young Bruckner with the essence of the baroque; in Steyr, in the *Stadtpfarrkirche*, the town's principal church, he was to receive the great impression of German gothic, another element which was later to find expression in his music. Musically, too, Steyr had two great things to offer him: the organ of the *Stadtpfarrkirche* on which he could improvise to his heart's content, and the contact with Karoline Eberstaller, the daughter of a French general, who had played piano duets with Schubert whenever he stayed in Steyr during the last years of his life. Karoline Eberstaller now introduced Bruckner to the romantic world of Franz Schubert. Together they played his music for piano duet and for two pianos, and thus a new facet was given to the musical vision of the young Bruckner. St. Florian, Steyr and Enns; baroque and gothic; Bach and Schubert: these are the roots of Bruckner's music, to which the great Italian masters of polyphony were to be added. The much later and often-quoted influence of Wagnerian music and its harmonies was merely an addition, an opulent colouring superimposed on fundamental conceptions which by that time were already firmly implanted in Bruckner's musical outlook.

The years in Kronstorf also saw several more attempts at composition: a *Tafellied* for male chorus (1843), a *Libera* in F (about 1843), a *Tantum ergo* in D (1843), a Choral Mass for Maundy Thursday[1] (1844) and a Cantata *Vergissmeinnicht* for soli, mixed chorus and piano (1845). Three further compositions from this period (a Litany, a *Salve Regina* and a Requiem) are no longer extant. It must be admitted, however (and this also applies to the majority of the compositions from the second St. Florian period, 1845–55), that these works bear little witness of greatness to come. They are neatly written pieces and show the thoroughness with which Bruckner absorbed the craft of composition, but the only Bruckner characteristic to be found in them is his devoutness in all things religious. Only one small idiosyncracy is apparent in the Cantata *Vergissmeinnicht*: Bruckner revised the work twice, so that it exists in three versions. This is the first evidence of the urge for continuous revision and re-revision which in later years was to become almost an obsession with Bruckner and which has created such an enormous problem in the textual clarification of his scores. All in all, Bruckner must have worked amazingly hard during those years, for apart from the regular routine of his daily work, as well as his lessons, his organ and piano practice and his composing, he also had to prepare himself for the second examination which every assistant teacher had to pass four years after obtaining the initial teacher's certificate from the *Präparandie*. Nevertheless, in May 1845 Bruckner passed this new examination, again with great success, and in the musical part of the examination he amazed his old friend and teacher Dürrnberger by the excellence of his contrapuntal improvisation on the organ. By all accounts Bruckner's improvisations at that time were infinitely superior to the compositions which he committed to paper, and it is a matter of everlasting regret that this glorious music is irrevocably lost to posterity.

St. Florian

At about the same time a vacancy occurred at St. Florian, and on the strength

[1] This Choral Mass, being specially composed for Maundy Thursday, contains a setting of the *Christus factus est*, the text which Bruckner was to set to music on two further occasions, in 1879 and 1884.

St. Florian, the Emperor's Gallery

of having passed this latest examination Bruckner obtained the post as 'first official assistant teacher in the parish school of St. Florian for the second big classroom'. On 25 September 1845 he returned to its cloistered walls, and there he was to remain for ten years, until December 1855. He moved into lodgings in the house of the headmaster Bogner where he had lived when a schoolboy, and initially he was completely absorbed by his teaching activities, music remaining his spare time occupation, and like his religion, his spiritual support. Nevertheless, for two hours a day he practised the organ under the supervision of the organist Kattinger, and during the first year of his stay at St. Florian he continued his regular visits to Enns for further theoretical studies with Zenetti. His main preoccupation at that time was Bach's organ music, and he often went to Linz to hear recitals. It was in Linz that he heard and became particularly

St. Florian, the house of the headmaster Bogner where Bruckner lived 1836–40 and 1845–56

attracted to the music of Mendelssohn. From contemporary reports it appears that the influence of Mendelssohn's style made itself felt in his organ improvisations, and there are also traces of it in some of his choral compositions of that period. These early years at St. Florian brought forth a number of works, many of them naturally enough of a religious nature, but also some small organ pieces and male choruses. Some of these latter compositions came into being through the formation of a male quartet in which Bruckner sang first bass. The second bass was the St. Florian gardener, Johann Nepomuk Hueber, who later married Bruckner's sister Rosalie and eventually settled with her and his family in Vöcklabruck where Bruckner often came to visit them from Vienna. But throughout this time music, although his first and greatest love, was still something of a 'hobby' with Bruckner, and he had not yet recognised his true vocation.

From all accounts these years were rich in friendship and happy personal relationships for Bruckner, and one of his great admirers was the judicial actuary Franz Sailer, godfather to Bruckner's brother Ignaz. In 1847 Sailer bought a Bösendorfer grand piano, and it was Bruckner's greatest joy to improvise on that magnificent instrument. One day he exclaimed: 'If only I could afford to buy myself such a piano!' Little did he know how soon, and under what sad circumstances, he was to become the possessor of the instrument. In September 1848 Sailer died suddenly of a heart attack and bequeathed the piano to Anton Bruckner in whose possession it remained until his dying day and who composed every one of his works on it.[1] But Sailer's death had another, more far-reaching effect. As a token of his gratitude Bruckner composed a Requiem Mass for his departed friend, the Requiem in D minor, which may certainly be looked upon as the first of his compositions which retains its validity to the present day, and may justifiably be described as the first precursor of the 'great' Bruckner.

1848, the 'year of revolutions', produced a great number of changes, and their effect was felt even in the calm of St. Florian when Kattinger, the organist who also held a judicial post, was transferred to Kremsmünster. Bruckner was appointed provisional organist, and the years 1848–49 mark the beginning of the transition from Bruckner the teacher to Bruckner the musician, a transition which was to be completed when he went to Linz in 1855.

During these transitional years Bruckner was full of indecision and consequently found little peace and happiness within himself. This was one of his characteristic traits which showed itself again during the last years of his time in Linz, when he had to make the decision between Linz and Vienna. Two opposing poles attracted him and pulled him to and fro: his love for his music on the one hand, and his strong desire for some sort of security on the other. In this latter respect he went to lengths which, in retrospect, seem extreme to the point of the ludicrous, for at one time he even made application to be admitted to the civil service in a clerical capacity. It was both his good fortune as well as the good fortune of posterity that his efforts in that direction were of no avail. Then there was another problem, a problem which recurred throughout Bruckner's life with almost monotonous regularity and frequency: he fell in love, this time with Louise, the daughter of the headmaster Bogner with whom he lodged, and once again his love was rejected. To this love-affair we owe some minor compositions, songs and short piano pieces, which are of small intrinsic value and of little interest except as museum pieces.

In 1851, according to Max Auer, Bruckner received his official appointment as organist at St. Florian, and in consequence he began at last to emerge as a

[1] This piano, together with the rest of Bruckner's few items of furniture, now stands in the 'Bruckner Room' in St. Florian.

composer. His compositions were requested for the regular musical needs of the community as well as for special occasions, and as he had to divide his time between his duties as teacher, as organist and as composer, voices began to be raised in some quarters claiming that he was neglecting his teaching activities. Any accusation of this nature touched Bruckner deeply, for he was of a most conscientious nature, and he did not rest until he was given a certificate by one of the priests of St. Florian, vouching for his character, his behaviour and the conscientious manner in which he discharged his various duties. But all these events did not serve to put Bruckner in a happier frame of mind, especially as during that time many of his more intimate circle of friends either died or left St. Florian. He wrote to his friend, Josef Seiberl[1]:

> 'You see how terribly everything has changed. All alone I sit in my little room in deepest melancholy.'

His only refuge and consolation in those days was his faith in God and his love for his music, and the combination of the two, in 1852, brought forth the 114th Psalm for five-part chorus and three trombones. Although the work is not of the same musical importance as the Requiem of 1848–49, it does bear unmistakable traces of his later compositions, especially in the double fugue towards the end which culminates in a truly Brucknerian *unisono*. During the following two years Bruckner's days were more than filled with his studies, his compositions and his duties.

On 24 March 1854 Michael Arneth, whose friendship had meant so much to Bruckner, died. For the funeral Bruckner composed a male chorus, again accompanied by three trombones, *Vor Arneths Grab* (By Arneth's Grave), as well as a *Libera* in F minor which was performed at the conclusion of the Requiem Mass. Arneth's successor, Friedrich Mayr, was enthroned on 14 September 1854, and this enthronement was the occasion of the first performance of the largest and most important work Bruckner had so far composed, the *Missa solemnis* in B flat minor. Although Bruckner used in this work sketches from his Kronstorf days, these were considerably elaborated, and for the first time he shows that he has begun to master large-scale form as well as the intricacies of writing for a full orchestra. Naturally the work does not yet measure up to the great Masses which Bruckner was to compose in later years, but nevertheless the *Missa solemnis*, contrary to many of the other compositions of those days, is even nowadays worthy of performance. It was received with great acclaim, yet there was one drop of bitterness in Bruckner's cup: all the guests were invited to the banquet following the enthronement ceremony except him—this would have been against monastic etiquette. Bruckner was most hurt, and the story goes that he went to the local inn, the *Gasthaus Sperl*, ordered a five-course meal with three different wines and settled down to it in solitude with the words: '*That* Mass deserves it!'

Bruckner always set great store by testimonials and certificates of all kinds, and at this period of his life (he was now 30 years old) he acquired two further

[1] Seiberl succeeded Bruckner as organist at St. Florian in 1855.

Wrought-iron gates in the Great Staircase

Anton Bruckner in 1854 (1863 according to H. Schöny)

such 'diplomas'. In October 1854 he passed an organ examination in Vienna, in the course of which he improvised a double fugue, and in January 1855 he sat for an examination in Linz to qualify as a high school teacher, which he passed with 'very good' in all principal subjects. Armed with these certificates Bruckner's sense of security increased immediately, for now he felt that he had something to fall back on in times of need, but they did not satisfy him with regard to his competence as a composer.

In April 1855 the composer and organist Robert Führer, a somewhat dubious character[1], came to St. Florian, and Bruckner immediately showed him the score of the *Missa solemnis*, played a bit on the organ and—asked for a certificate. Führer gave him a splendid testimonial but advised him at the same time to study the strict rules of harmony and counterpoint with Simon Sechter in Vienna.[2] Remembering that Mayr, after hearing the *Missa solemnis*, had made a similar remark, Bruckner became so struck with the idea that in July 1855 he made the journey to Vienna. Sechter, having also been shown the *Missa solemnis*, accepted him as a pupil immediately. Sechter was so impressed with Bruckner's talent that he advised him to leave the seclusion of St. Florian, a piece of advice which served to increase the torment of restlessness and indecision that raged within Bruckner. This may be the reason why he secretly applied for the vacant position of cathedral organist in Olmütz (now Olomouc in Czechoslovakia), but when the prior came to hear of this application, Bruckner earned himself a most severe reprimand. The matter in itself is unimportant, except that it had an amusing sequel. In November 1855 the cathedral organist in Linz, Wenzel Pranghofer, died, and 13 November was the date fixed for the examination of candidates for this vacancy. When on that day the organ tuner came from Linz to St. Florian, he fully expected Bruckner to be in Linz to compete for the post, for even then Bruckner was known as one of Austria's finest organists, and he was very surprised to find him in St. Florian. After much persuasion Bruckner went to Linz, but only to call on his old teacher Dürrnberger. Dürrnberger immediately assumed that Bruckner had come to compete for the post, but Bruckner replied: 'How can I! I haven't told them anything about it at St. Florian—and what do you think they would say to me if I applied for the post behind their backs!' However, Bruckner accompanied Dürrnberger to the cathedral to listen to the other candidates, Engelbert Lanz and Raimund Hain. When neither of these had solved the task given to them—improvising on a set theme and concluding with a fugue—to the satisfaction of the board of examiners, Dürrnberger went up to Bruckner who was absorbed in prayer and said to him: 'Tonerl, you *must* play!' Then, at last, Bruckner climbed up to the organ loft and began improvising on the theme, quite simply at first, then with increasing complexity and finally culminating in a grandiose fugue. The acclamation which he received left no room for doubt as to who

1 Among other things, Führer added trumpet and timpani parts to Schubert's Mass in G and claimed it as his original composition.

2 This, incidentally, is the same Simon Sechter whom Schubert approached two weeks before his death for lessons in counterpoint.

Linz, Hauptplatz *with the old cathedral*

was to be the future cathedral organist in Linz, and when Bruckner, with much trepidation, confessed to Mayr that he had taken part in the competition and had been awarded the post, the prior patted him on the back and said: 'That is a different matter, and I don't blame you! I could not possibly hold you back from such an improvement in your position. Go to Linz, and go with God's blessing.' There was still Bruckner's eternal indecision to be overcome. In fact, before finally accepting the post, Bruckner made sure of a line of retreat by asking for an assurance that his old position at St. Florian would be kept open for him for a period of two years. There was also some minor difficulty about his somewhat undignified manner of dressing on official visits, but all these small details were soon smoothed out, and after a moving farewell from all his friends and pupils at St. Florian Bruckner took up his duties in Linz in December 1855.[1]

It was thus not until his thirty-second year that Bruckner became a full-time musician, and the following twelve years until he moved to Vienna in the summer of 1868 were to be amongst the most formative years of his entire life, for just as the St. Florian period saw the transformation from the teacher to the

[1] The official document confirming his appointment was not made out until April 1856.

musician, so the Linz period brought about that greatest and most vital transformation from Bruckner the organist to Bruckner the symphonist.

Linz

Throughout his life Bruckner's constant complaint was that he lacked time, yet even in this busy life the period in Linz must have comprised the years when he worked his hardest. First and foremost there were his duties as organist at the two churches, the cathedral and the *Pfarrkirche*, together with many hours of daily practice to perfect himself as an organist. In addition he gave piano lessons and spent up to seven hours a day working at his theoretical studies, which he continued by correspondence with Simon Sechter in Vienna. How hard he worked, and how seriously he took these studies, is shown by a letter from Simon Sechter, normally a very hard task-master, when on one occasion Bruckner had sent him no less than seventeen exercise books filled with 'homework':

> 'I really must admonish you to take more care of yourself and to allow yourself sufficient relaxation. I can assure you that I am fully convinced of your assiduity and eagerness and I do not wish your health to suffer under too great a mental strain. I feel constrained to tell you that I have never had a a more dedicated pupil.'

Yet in the midst of all this activity Bruckner also found time to become a very active member of the Linz choral association, the *Liedertafel 'Frohsinn'*, whose conductor he was to become in 1860, nor did he lack a certain amount of social life. He made many friends in Linz, foremost amongst them Moritz von Mayfeld and his wife, and the two Weinwurm brothers, Alois and Rudolf. The friendship with Rudolf Weinwurm became particularly intimate, especially after Rudolf had moved to Vienna and did much there to help Bruckner on his various visits to the Austrian capital and to prepare the ground for Bruckner's own move to Vienna in 1868.

During the period of his studies with Sechter Bruckner customarily travelled to Vienna twice a year, usually during Lent and during Advent, these being the periods when the organ in church had to remain silent, and on those occasions he spent all his time with his teacher, who soon became also a personal friend. Each year Bruckner had to pass an examination with Sechter, and on one occasion, in July 1858, he also sat for an examination in harmony, figured bass and organ playing. In the ensuing testimonial Sechter states that Bruckner 'shows much experience and versatility in improvisation and in developing a theme and may therefore be counted as one amongst the finest organists.' Although the performance in the *Piaristenkirche*, being in the nature of an examination, was a private one, the Viennese critic Ludwig Speidel was present and gave Bruckner a glowing report in the *Wiener Zeitung* of 24 July—a fact which greatly enhanced his reputation in Linz.

In 1861 Bruckner concluded his studies with Sechter, during the course of which he had covered every conceivable field of contrapuntal writing, and once again Sechter furnished him with a splendid testimonial. With all his pupils Sechter had one iron rule, a rule which later on Bruckner also enforced with his own students: First the theory, *then* free creative composition. This explains the almost complete absence of works from Bruckner's pen during the years 1856–60. In 1856, apart from one or two minor works (a small-scale piano piece and a song) he only composed an *Ave Maria* for St. Florian as a kind of farewell gift, and in 1860 he completed the 146th Psalm for soli, chorus and orchestra which presumably he had already begun in St. Florian. However, his appointment as conductor of the *Liedertafel* '*Frohsinn*' in succession to A. M. Storch in November 1860 automatically gave rise to several new compositions, all the more so as this appointment coincided more or less with the conclusion of his studies with Sechter. The first occasion arose through the death of the wife of one of the committee members of the *Liedertafel*, Josef Hafferl. Bruckner made use of the same poem which had furnished the text for *Vor Arneths Grab* (1854), this time omitting the last verse. He composed an entirely new setting for male chorus, and entitled the work *Am Grabe*. It was the first work by Bruckner to be heard in Linz. The *Liedertafel* sang it at the funeral, and the *Linzer Zeitung* commented: 'The entire composition is imbued with tender emotion and immovable faith in God.' This was followed by a work which may easily have been written in gratitude for having successfully completed his studies with Sechter: the seven-part *a-cappella Ave Maria*. With this composition he proved that he had completely absorbed the art of contrapuntal writing, and even in retrospect it stands out as a work of truly Brucknerian mastery. It was first performed in Linz under Bruckner on 15 May 1861 during a religious service at which, with the *Liedertafel*, he also performed a Mass by Antonio Lotti.

A word must be said at this point about certain aspects of Bruckner's private life during these years at Linz. One of his constant sources of strength and joy was the friendship of his immediate superior, Bishop Franz Josef Rudigier. From the very first Bishop Rudigier recognised Bruckner's exceptional gifts as an organist, and came frequently to the cathedral to sit alone and listen while Bruckner was immersed in his organ practice. Whenever they met in the street he favoured Bruckner with a particularly friendly greeting, and to Bruckner this warmth of human and artistic understanding was a great solace. In another respect, however, Bruckner's life at that time was less happy. He was living a bachelor's existence and longed for the physical and spiritual comforts of a real home. Several times he attempted to persuade his mother to come to Linz, but she always declined, saying that town life was not for her. Her death in 1860 brought yet another great grief into Bruckner's life. It affected him so deeply, in fact, that he arranged to have a photograph taken of her on her death bed, and this photograph accompanied Bruckner throughout the rest of his life, though usually it was hidden behind a small velvet curtain as the constant sight of it upset him too much. The obvious solution to this

Linz, Pfarrgasse where Bruckner lived for some time

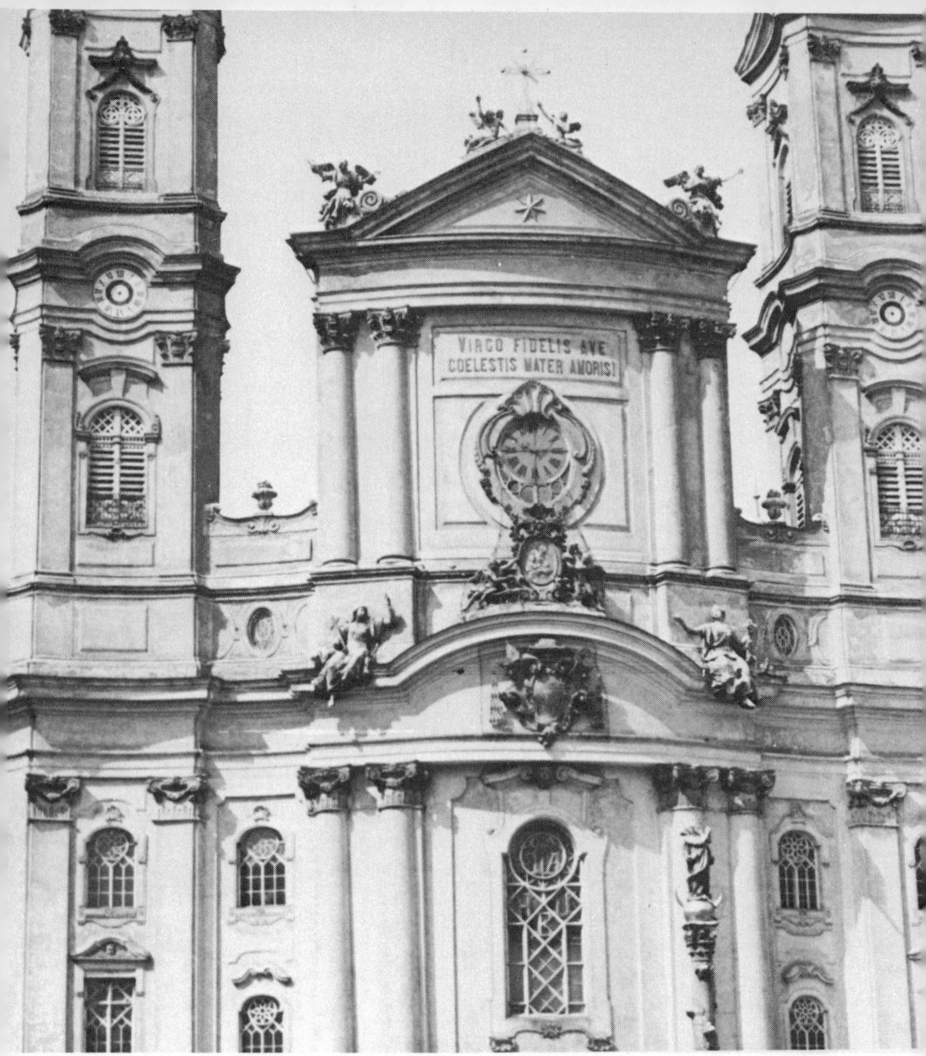

Façade of the Piaristenkirche, *Vienna*

problem of his solitude would have been to marry, and throughout his life Bruckner's thoughts turned frequently in this direction. His heart was very easily inflamed, particularly by girls between 16 and 19, but owing to the purity of his entire character and the firmness of his religious beliefs any connection with a member of the opposite sex outside marriage was out of the question for him. Countless times he fell in love, proposed, and was rejected. Much as he was liked as a person and friend, his outward appearance and his somewhat

ANTON BRUCKNER
UNTERZOG SICH AM 21. NOVEMBER 1861
AN DER ORGEL DIESER KIRCHE
DER PRAKTISCHEN KOMPOSITIONSPRÜFUNG.
JOHANN HERBECK, DER SPÄTERE HOFKAPELLMEISTER,
FASSTE DAS ERGEBNIS IN DIE DENKWÜRDIGEN WORTE:
„ER HÄTTE UNS PRÜFEN SOLLEN"
1961
Bezirksvorstehung Josefstadt - Josefstädter Heimatmuseum

Plaque on the Piaristenkirche *commemorating Bruckner's examination in composition*

awkward manner seemed to preclude him from being considered as a suitable husband. It is a matter which has been widely discussed by all writers on the subject of Bruckner and will be mentioned again when we consider his character as a whole. As far as his Linz years are concerned, his lonely life was relieved when his sister Maria Anna came to live with him in 1866. She also moved with him to Vienna in 1868 and remained with him until her death in 1870.

During the year 1861 Bruckner, now free from the enormous amount of work which he had had to do for Sechter, threw himself into a new fever of activity as conductor of the *Liedertafel* '*Frohsinn*'. In rehearsals he was exceedingly demanding and soon raised the standard of the choir to such a level that he could safely participate with it in choral competitions in Krems and Nürnberg. Wherever the *Liedertafel* made an appearance it received enthusiastic praise, and one of the most important aspects of this for Bruckner personally was the recognition shown him in Nürnberg by Johann Herbeck, then conductor of the *Wiener Männergesangsverein* and later *Hofkapellmeister* in Vienna, who up until his death was to be one of the staunchest supporters and promoters of Bruckner's music.

One episode from this period of his work with the *Liedertafel* is worth mentioning here. Bruckner always aimed at precision and good enunciation in his rehearsals, but one thing he particularly insisted on was a truly delicate *pianissimo*. On one occasion, in a work by Schumann, he kept repeating a certain *piano* passage over and over again, exclaiming with annoyance: 'It still sounds like a trumpet!' until the members of the choir got tired of the procedure and decided that at the next rehearsal they would not sing at all in the passage in question. When it came to the point, the choir fell silent, and Bruckner, hearing the music with his inner ear, went on conducting, smiling blissfully and saying: 'Now it's right!' An amusing story, yet also a very clear indication to all interpreters of his music as to what Bruckner meant by *pianissimo*!

Bruckner's conductorship of the *Liedertafel* came to an end in September 1861 as a result of an unfortunate occurrence while the choir was in Nürnberg for the choral festival. Once again he was much taken by a girl. Her name was Olga, and she was a waitress in a restaurant where Bruckner and his singers often went in the evenings to drink wine. The singers, in their wine-happy mood, decided to play a joke on Bruckner. They lured him into an empty room and sent Olga, very seductively dressed, to join him there. For this type of joke, however, Bruckner had no sense of humour whatsoever. He fled from the room in confusion and anger and refused to have anything further to do with the choir. In a letter to his friend Weinwurm he writes: 'In September I was so insulted by the *Liedertafel* that I had to resign.' It so happened that at about that time the conductorship of the *Dommusikverein und Mozarteum* in Salzburg became vacant, and Bruckner immediately applied for the post. But here he came up against various internal intrigues, as was to happen to him so often in his life, and the position was given to one Hans Schläger.

As always when he suffered a disappointment, Bruckner took refuge in his work. Two minor compositions date from this period, a Fugue in D minor for organ and the *Afferentur regi* for mixed chorus and three trombones, but in the main his energies and his time were absorbed in preparations for yet another examination. In October he applied to the Vienna Conservatorium for a diploma which would qualify him as a 'Teacher of Harmony and Counterpoint at Conservatoria', sending in his reports from Sechter as well as some contrapuntal exercises and free compositions. The main part of the examination was to consist of a free improvisation on a given theme, including a fugue, on the organ. Bruckner chose the organ of the *Piaristenkirche* in Vienna, and there, on 22 November 1861, the examination took place in the presence of Joseph Hellmesberger, Johann Herbeck, Simon Sechter, Otto Dessoff and a school inspector, Becker. First Herbeck asked Sechter to write down a theme. He wrote four bars, which Herbeck then passed to Dessoff requesting him to add to them. When Dessoff refused, considering the theme to be quite long enough, Herbeck himself added a further four bars, at which Dessoff exclaimed: 'How cruel!' The theme was given to Bruckner, who spent a few minutes meditating over it. This was interpreted as evidence of inability by the examining committee and led to some amusement, but then Bruckner began with an introduction based on fragments of the theme, led into a fugue which began with a statement of the entire theme in the bass and brought it to an immense climax, culminating on a pedal point. The effect on the examining committee was overwhelming and their reaction spontaneous, and Herbeck summed up the result in the famous words: 'He should have examined us!'

Bruckner was now an acknowledged master of harmony, counterpoint and free improvisation, yet there was one field where he still felt the need for further instruction: the principles of musical form and orchestration. To this end destiny appears to have sent him the right man at the right moment in the person of Otto Kitzler, first 'cellist of the municipal theatre in Linz, a man ten years Bruckner's junior. Bruckner placed himself into his hands unreservedly and once again became an eager and assiduous pupil. During the first month of his studies with Kitzler he composed some minor vocal works—one for the male choir of his friend Alois Weinwurm, and another for Bishop Rudigier to celebrate the laying of the foundation stone of the new Linz cathedral—but from then onwards it was the orchestra that dominated his attention. Kitzler based his teaching partly on the textbooks of formal analysis and orchestration, but mainly on the living music of the great masters, particularly Beethoven and the then 'modern' Mendelssohn. The change for Bruckner must have been tremendous, coming as he did from the dry and academic method of Sechter's contrapuntal teaching, to plunge now into the wealth of so much great and vital music. Once again his studies gave rise to a number of 'composition exercises': a String Quartet in C minor, two Marches for military band (although one of these, the *Apollo-Marsch*, is of doubtful authenticity); and his first attempts at writing for large orchestra: a March in D minor (which is interesting because it contains a passage that was to recur much later in the Finale of the Eighth Symphony) and three small-scale orchestral pieces. Towards the end of 1862, when Bruckner's studies with Kitzler had got as far as the sonata form, a decisive event occurred. Kitzler had decided to give the first performance in Linz of Wagner's *Tannhäuser*, and together with Bruckner he studied the score of the work, which was an eye-opener indeed for Bruckner! First and foremost it demonstrated to him that the creative impulse is greater than the hallowed rules of the classroom, that the creative genius has the right, even at times the duty to break these rules. And then he found a wealth of harmonies, harmonies that he had dreamt of but had never dared to use. As Auer writes, *Tannhäuser* freed Bruckner from the shackles of Sechter's strict teaching and gave him the licence to use those chromatic harmonies and enharmonic changes against which Sechter had fought with such acerbity. Yet it must be remembered that this great impact of Wagner's music came to Bruckner at a time when he was virtually at the end of his 'apprenticeship' as a composer. Up until his thirty-ninth year he had neither heard nor seen one single note of Wagner's compositions. All the main foundations on which Bruckner's great work was to rise had been laid, and this contact with *Tannhäuser* merely added to and enriched something which was already essentially established. Perhaps the nearest approach to the truth would be to say that, as a kindred spirit, Wagner provided the stimulus which allowed ideas that were latent within Bruckner himself to pour forth. We should not overlook the fact that several of Bruckner's earlier compositions contain

Vienna, interior of the Hofburgkapelle

passages which strike one today as being distinctly Wagnerian in flavour, and at that time Wagner's music was completely unknown to him.

Bruckner's studies with Kitzler gave rise to his first two major orchestral works, the Overture in G Minor (completed in January 1863) and the Symphony in F minor (completed in May 1863). Bruckner considered these works as mere test pieces, to prove to himself as well as to Kitzler that he had absorbed all the subject matter of Kitzler's teaching, and in later years he rejected the F minor Symphony out of hand as being nothing more than a student exercise. These two works were followed by a composition for double chorus and orchestra, the 112th Psalm, and now at long last Bruckner felt that he had mastered both choral and orchestral composition. During the summer of 1863, in consequence, he allowed himself the luxury of a holiday, most of which was spent in the *Salzkammergut*, and afterwards began to concentrate on serious composition. The first work of this new era was a male chorus with orchestra, the *Germanenzug*, and this, as Bruckner himself once said, he considered his first real composition. It was also the first work of Bruckner's to appear in print. In September 1863 Bruckner paid his first visit to Munich on the occasion of the 11th Music Festival, and with his return to Linz in October the first great creative period began: the Symphony in D minor (1863–64),[1] the Mass No. 1 in D minor (1864), the Symphony No. 1 in C minor (1865–66), the Mass No. 2 in E minor (1866) and the Mass No. 3 in F minor (1867–68), with a number of smaller, mainly vocal, compositions interspersed between these large-scale works. The D minor Symphony, which Bruckner revised in 1869, is the one on the score of which, one year before his death, he made the pencilled remarks 'Only an attempt' and 'Totally invalid', yet that he did not reject it completely is proved by the fact that he assigned it a number—No. 0. It was first performed in 1924, on the centenary of Bruckner's birth. Although the symphony does not, of course, measure up to the nine 'great' symphonies, it is nevertheless a work of considerable intrinsic worth and individuality and fully deserves to appear more frequently in concert programmes instead of being consigned to a sort of musicological lumber room.

In 1864, at the age of 40, Bruckner wrote what can be regarded as his first 'masterpiece': the Mass in D minor. It is a work of great beauty, exuding a religious fervour and intensity which transcends the boundaries of a particular creed, and at the same time it is of the utmost daring in its form and in its harmonic and melodic progressions. It may seem astonishing that Bruckner should so suddenly have attained such a sublime level, but the answer is simple. As Bruckner himself said: 'I didn't dare before.'[2] It must have meant a great wrench for Bruckner to liberate himself from the fetters of that authority, the

[1] This is the date assigned to the work by Auer, Haas and Nowak. J. V. Wöss and others, however, are of the opinion that Bruckner only made preliminary sketches in 1863–64, and that the actual composition of the Symphony took place in 1869, between the two C minor Symphonies now known as No. 1 and No. 2, the year assigned by Auer, etc. to the revision of the work. (See Wöss's Foreword to the score published by Universal Edition, 1924.)

[2] See Nowak, *Anton Bruckner: Musik und Leben*, Vienna, 1964.

SYM. #7

authority of his teachers and their theoretical rules, to which he had adhered for so long, and with such devotion and respect. The Mass was originally intended to be performed on 18 August 1864, the birthday of the Austrian Emperor, but as it was not completed in time it was first heard in Linz Cathedral on 20 November of that year. The reception accorded to it was such that a special *Concert spirituel* was arranged for a second, this time a concert performance, in December. On the personal level the performances of the Mass resulted in a great deepening and strengthening of the bonds of friendship between Bruckner and Moritz von Mayfeld, who was later to be so influential in urging Bruckner towards his true vocation—the symphony.

During 1864 Bruckner had a series of unhappy encounters with members of the fair sex, and in his misery he wrote to Weinwurm proposing to emigrate to Russia or Mexico[1], but these were passing fancies. Soon he was back at work, and in January 1865 the Symphony No. 1 in C minor was begun, though in May the composition was interrupted by another visit to Munich. Wagner had invited a great number of artists to be present at the first performance of *Tristan und Isolde*, and such an invitation was, for Bruckner, equivalent to a royal command. There he met many famous musicians of his day, among them Hans von Bülow, who conducted the performance, and Wagner himself. He showed the beginnings of his symphony to Bülow, who professed himself to be enthusiastic, but Bruckner was too timid to show it to Wagner. Nevertheless the foundation stone of a lifelong friendship between Bruckner and Wagner was laid. It is interesting to note that Bruckner used a piano score *without text* to study *Tristan*, proof that his only interest was the actual music and that the dramatic content of the work was of no concern to him. This is also borne out by a later incident, when he went to hear *Die Walküre*. He is reported to have asked someone after the performance: 'Tell me, why did they burn the woman at the end?' Surely no one who so completely and utterly misses the dramatic point of Wagner's *Gesamtkunstwerk* can ever be termed a 'Wagnerian' in the true sense of the word!

In June 1865 Bruckner gave the first performance of his *Germanenzug* during a choral festival in Linz. Owing to internal intrigues he was only awarded the second prize, a fact which filled him with dismay, but an important result of this performance was that he made the acquaintance of Eduard Hanslick, the critic and all-powerful musical dictator of Vienna, for whom he also improvised on the organ. Considering the hate and spite with which Hanslick was to persecute Bruckner in years to come, it seems strange to see him in 1865 giving Bruckner friendly advice and guidance and presenting him with a signed photograph.

In January 1866 the C minor Symphony was completed and rehearsals began immediately. Owing to various circumstances, however, these had to be abandoned, and more than two years were to elapse before the symphony eventually came before the public in May 1868. The ensuing months were in the nature of a creative pause and brought forth but a few occasional composi-

[1] For some strange reason Mexico always held a peculiar fascination for Bruckner.

tions: three works for male chorus and a piece for violin and piano entitled *Abendklänge*. During this period Bruckner's heart was once again fired with love, this time for 17-year-old Josefine Lang. Among his many 'flames' she deserves special mention, since she was undoubtedly one of his deepest loves. Again he was rejected, the reason given being the discrepancy in age, and it was to relieve his subsequent unhappiness that his sister Maria Anna came to join him in Linz and make a home for him. His main refuge and solace, however, was as always in his music and in his faith, and out of the combination of these came his Mass No. 2 in E minor in the autumn of 1866. Written for eight-part chorus with wind accompaniment, it is unique not only within the scope of Bruckner's own work, but also within the entire musical output of his time. A masterpiece of contrapuntal architecture, it looks back to the great age of Palestrina and the vocal polyphony of the sixteenth and seventeenth centuries, and yet in its harmonic turns and its devout expressiveness it is true and original Bruckner.

Throughout his life Bruckner tended to oscillate between moods of optimism and gaiety and fits of gloom and depression, a characteristic which, as has been suggested earlier, he may possibly have inherited from his mother. Although outwardly he appears to have had little cause for unhappiness apart from his perennial disappointments in affairs of the heart, since his Mass in E minor was completed and Herbeck had performed the Mass in D minor at the *Hofkapelle* in Vienna (a signal honour for any composer), yet the earlier part of 1867 found Bruckner in a state of nervous anxiety and severe depression. Soon matters came to such a pass that medical treatment was necessary, and he spent three months—8 May to 8 August 1867—in a sanatorium in Bad Kreuzen where he underwent a cold water cure. His letters to Weinwurm and others from this period give clear evidence of his state of mind: he speaks of impending madness, hints at suicide, and regards himself as completely forsaken by his friends. During this period he also showed signs of numeromania, for he felt an inner compulsion to count anything and everything—the leaves of a tree, the stars, grains of sand. Traces of this may be found later, in his insistence on numbering bars and periodicity in his scores. However, the cure proved effective, and in August he returned to Linz, restored in mental and physical health.

In September 1867 his friend and former teacher Simon Sechter died, an event which was to have far-reaching consequences for Bruckner. Although his great hope of obtaining the appointment at the *Hofkapelle*, for which he made an immediate application, was not to be realised, Herbeck decided then and there that Bruckner was the man to succeed Sechter as professor of harmony and counterpoint at the Conservatorium, so that Sechter's death was in fact the direct cause for Bruckner's move to Vienna in 1868. However, before that took place Bruckner was to experience two further disappointments in Linz. His application for the position at the *Hofkapelle* as well as another application to the Vienna University, concerning the creation of a lectureship in harmony and counterpoint, were rejected, and a further performance of his D minor

Mass in Linz did not receive the same unreserved praise from his friend Mayfeld as three years earlier. As if in compensation, he was re-appointed conductor of the *Liedertafel 'Frohsinn'* in January 1868, and the 4 April of that year was to be an historic day. In a concert commemorating the foundation of the *Liedertafel* the choir, under Bruckner, gave the first performance of the Finale of Act III of *Die Meistersinger von Nürnberg*. Wagner himself had made the suggestion when Bruckner had enquired about a suitable choral work, and it shows the esteem in which Wagner must have held Bruckner. To Bruckner and Linz went the credit of performing a section of the music drama before the work as such had yet been staged.

One month later Linz was to hear the first performance of Bruckner's Symphony No. 1 in C minor. Owing to the unusual technical difficulties of the work the performance was far from perfect, but nevertheless it was a great success with the audience, and Moritz von Mayfeld in the *Linzer Zeitung* gave unstinted praise to the work. Even Hanslick mentioned the performance in the Vienna press, concluding: 'There are rumours that Bruckner is to join the staff of the Vienna Conservatorium. If these should be correct, we may well congratulate the institution.'

Throughout the years 1867–68 Bruckner was at work on his Mass No. 3 in F minor, the last Mass he was to compose and considered by many to be his greatest. He applied himself to this task with the utmost fervour and, by all accounts, must at times have been in an almost ecstatic state, far removed from the realities of this world. It is understandable that during these years Bruckner wrote only a few other choral compositions apart from this enormous work, all the more so since the months spent in Bad Kreuzen sanatorium fell into the same period. The F minor Mass was the last work which Bruckner completed in Linz, shortly before he moved to Vienna.

The fact that within the space of four years, between autumn 1864 and autumn 1868, Bruckner conceived and composed these three great Masses and then never even considered writing another, has often been commented upon. Some writers have seen in it the 'proof' that Bruckner's religious fervour was on the decline, but this is decisively contradicted not only by the evidence of his own life and the reports of his friends and contemporaries, but also by the list of compositions written during the Vienna period, the last twenty-eight years of his life, which includes a number of very beautiful and deeply moving choral works of a liturgical nature as well as his great *Te Deum* of 1883–84 and the 150th Psalm of 1892. The answer surely lies in an entirely different direction. It must have become increasingly obvious to Bruckner that his true vocation was the symphony. Whereas in the days when he was still somewhat unsure of himself in this field he had felt the need for words, the text of the Mass, to express that which filled his entire being, in later years, as his powers of symphonic utterance increased, those very words which had originally served as an inspiration became a hindrance, and he was able to sing his *Gloria*, his *Credo* and his *Benedictus* in the wordless, all-embracing, absolute music of his gigantic symphonic movements.

The critic Eduard Hanslick

Johannes Brahms

Bruckner's last months in Linz, from May to July 1868, were again fraught with emotional disturbances. A renewed attempt to obtain the conductorship of the *Dommusikverein und Mozarteum* in Salzburg failed and merely brought him an honorary membership. Then, at Easter, Herbeck approached him with the offer of the professorship at the Vienna Conservatorium in succession to Sechter. As had happened at the time of the decisive move from St. Florian to Linz in 1855 Bruckner was again torn by indecision. He feared for his financial security, as his income in Linz was considerably higher than the salary offered him in Vienna, and in addition Bishop Rudigier had promised to try to assure him of a pension in his old age. The letters which Bruckner wrote at that time border on the pathetic, and it was only due to the continued urging and unfailing patience of his Viennese friends, in particular Rudolf Weinwurm and Herbeck himself, that in the end Bruckner accepted the position. What finally decided him was that Herbeck had not only succeeded in increasing the salary offered from 600 to 800 guilders, but had also extracted a promise that, if Bruckner came to Vienna, he would be appointed court organist *in Exspektanz*—an unpaid provisional appointment. Nevertheless, as before in St. Florian, Bruckner kept his line of retreat open, and it was only on 18 July 1870 that he officially resigned from his Linz posts.

Vienna

The move to Vienna took place in the summer of 1868, and together with his sister 'Nani' he moved into the *Höhne-Haus*, Währingerstrasse 41, which was to be the 'birth place' of the next four symphonies. On 1 October he took up his duties at the *Konservatorium der Gesellschaft der Musikfreunde* where he taught both theory (harmony and counterpoint) and organ. His first pupils included two young men who were later to become famous in their own right: Wladimir von Pachmann, the pianist, and Felix Mottl, the conductor. Mottl was the first of many pupils and students who later repaid their beloved teacher by their unrelenting efforts in promoting his compositions.

From the reports of his various pupils it is possible to gain a fairly clear picture of Bruckner's teaching methods. Two salient facts emerge immediately: Bruckner's strictness and severity in all matters connected with musical craft, be it in the field of theory, of composition or of organ playing, and the lively, natural manner in which he presented his subject. There was none of that arid atmosphere which so often surrounds the teaching of musical theory. Bruckner always knew how to make the subject attractive, and he appears to have been indefatigable in inventing amusing stories and anecdotes to make the subject under discussion more meaningful to his pupils, giving them parallels out of everyday life. Like his own teacher, Sechter, he forbade his students to indulge in individual liberties while engaged in their theoretical studies, and Mottl tells of the day he brought Bruckner a somewhat free solution of a harmony exercise. Bruckner looked at the homework and said in his broadest Austrian dialect: 'Here in school everything must go according to the rules, and you are not allowed to write one single forbidden note. But if you bring me something which is so strictly in accordance with the rules once you have finished your schooling, I'll throw you out!'

Besides his teaching at the Conservatorium Brukner also had to fulfil his unpaid duties as organist *in Exspektanz* at the *Hofkapelle*. During this period his organ playing must have been at its very peak, and he was chosen to go to Nancy in the spring of 1869 to participate in the series of recitals at the inauguration of the new organ in the church of St. Epvre. His playing of Bach and especially his free improvisations met with such acclaim that he was prevailed upon to go to Paris to play the organ in Notre-Dame. His audience included some of France's leading musicians—César Franck, Saint-Saëns, Auber, Gounod—and many years later they are said to have remembered Bruckner's improvisations with amazement and admiration. This was the first of Bruckner's two important journeys abroad as an organ virtuoso. The second was in 1871, when he was chosen to represent Austria in a series of concerts in which the leading organists of Europe were to play the new organ in the Royal Albert Hall in London. Reports about his success there are contradictory, but the fact remains that as a result of his recitals in the Albert Hall he was invited to give a further series of five recitals on the organ of the Crystal Palace, and these by all accounts led to the most enthusiastic ovations. It was envisaged that Bruckner should return to England in 1872 to give organ recitals in all the major English towns, but this plan never materialised, and although in later years he toyed with the idea of going to England on several occasions (England seems to have replaced Mexico in his dreams!) he never crossed the Channel again. It is also interesting to note that prior to his departure to England he is reputed to have said to his pupils: 'Well, I'm not going to bother much with Bach—I'll leave that to those who have no imagination. I'm going to do free improvisation on a theme.' This is a clear indication of Bruckner's own attitude to organ playing and explains why he, the master of the organ, left no compositions worth mentioning for the instrument.

Apart from the concert tours mentioned above, his first three years in Vienna were mainly taken up with his teaching work and his organ playing. Also, in order to further his general knowledge, Bruckner attended Hanslick's lectures on the history of music at the university during the year 1868–69. His financial position during these years was not ideal, but in 1868 he was granted a special sum of 500 guilders (and a further 400 guilders in 1870) by the Ministry of Education to assist him in the 'composition of major symphonic works'. Artistically and personally his life had its customary ups and downs. After his triumphs in France the *Liedertafel* in Linz made him an honorary member and Ansfelden made him an honorary citizen, but he suffered a great disappointment when Dessoff, the conductor of the Philharmonic Orchestra, rejected his Symphony No. 1, on account of its wildness and daring. Bruckner was very shaken by this rejection and spent much time in 1868–69 revising his D minor Symphony, No. 0. Apart from a work for male chorus with piano accompaniment, *Mitternacht*, the only new composition of those years was the *a capella*

Vienna, the house Währingerstrasse 41 where Bruckner lived 1868–76 and where he composed his 2nd, 3rd, 4th and 5th Symphonies

Gradual *Locus iste* of 1869, written for the dedication of the votive chapel of the new Linz Cathedral at which his E minor Mass was to have its first performance. The Mass, which he dedicated to Bishop Rudigier, was duly performed on the occasion, on 29 September 1869, and the Bishop was so moved by the work that he assured Bruckner of a burial place in the crypt of the chapel, an assurance which never came to fulfilment as Bruckner was to find his last resting place at St. Florian. In addition Bruckner received a present of 200 guilders for his Mass—one of the few times in his life that he received any financial reward for his work as a composer! His financial position took another turn for the better towards the end of 1870, when he was appointed teacher of piano, theory and organ at the Teacher Training College of St. Anna, but the additional work curtailed the time at his disposal for his own compositions still further and was also to lead to a most disagreeable incident on his return from London.

The early part of 1870 brought Bruckner another great sorrow, the loss of his favourite sister Maria Anna who had been looking after him for the last

The Crystal Palace, London (from an old engraving)

four years. For a while he was alone again, but soon on the recommendation of friends, one Katharina Kachelmayr became his housekeeper and remained with him right up to his death in 1896. 'Frau Kathi', as she appears to have been known by everyone, looked after Bruckner with a mixture of motherly care and amiable tyranny. The anecdotes about the frequent domestic squabbles between Frau Kathi and 'her' Bruckner are countless, but she looked after him well and chided him like a child when, immersed in his compositions, he occasionally forgot to eat his meals.

His London triumphs did much to restore Bruckner's self-confidence, which resulted in his starting work on the Symphony No. 2 in C minor. With this second symphony began the first of what Leopold Nowak so aptly terms Bruckner's 'two great creative waves'. It encompassed the years 1871–76 and comprised the compositions of Symphonies No. 2 (1871–72), No. 3 (1873), No. 4 (1874) and No. 5 (1875–76). It was followed by a period of revisions,

Royal Albert Hall, London (about 1895)

Bruckner at the organ. Silhouette by Otto Böhler

Bruckner conducting. Silhouette by Otto Böhler

1876–79, interspersed by several small-scale compositions. The second 'wave', from 1879 to 1887, began with the composition of the String Quintet in 1879 and included by way of major works the Symphonies No. 6 (1879–81), No. 7 (1881–83) and No. 8 (1884–87) as well as the *Te Deum* (1881 and 1883–84). This was again followed by a series of revisions undertaken between 1887 and 1891, and during the last five years of his life Bruckner concentrated almost entirely on his last symphony, No. 9, which was to remain unfinished. These last years also saw the composition of his last two major choral works, the 150th Psalm (1892) and *Helgoland* (1893).

The first of these creative periods is particularly noteworthy for its intensity. In less than five years Bruckner, in the midst of all his teaching activities (and he gave a great many lessons, as can be seen from his diary entries), conceived and composed four immense symphonies, culminating in the contrapuntal masterpiece of the Finale of the 5th Symphony. No other compositions whatsoever date from this period, and when one considers that, with the exception of the Symphony No. 2, Bruckner never heard a performance of any of his symphonies before starting work on the next, and moreover that the date marking the beginning of composition of one symphony coincides fairly closely with the completion date of its precursor, there can be no doubt about the unshakable faith which Bruckner had in his vocation as a symphonist. All idle talk about his 'uncertainty' and 'lack of self-assurance' must be silenced by these facts.

On his return from London, the inner peace which Bruckner had acquired through his triumphs was rapidly shattered, for he found that during his absence a disciplinary action had been started against him on the grounds that he had addressed one of his girl students at St. Anna as *lieber Schatz*—'my darling' or 'sweetheart'. Bruckner had used the term of endearment in an innocent, paternal manner, but a mountain had been made out of a molehill, and although the matter ended with a complete exculpation Bruckner was much embittered by it and asked to be relieved of any further activities in the female section of the Teacher Training College. However, this unpleasantness had little effect on his creative work. In fact throughout his life his composing was hardly ever affected by the external vicissitudes of his life: only *musical* disappointments had a deep and far-reaching effect on his work as a composer, resulting in those endless hours of revision with which so much of his time and energy was to be wasted.

Virtually the whole of 1872 was spent working on the Symphony No. 2. The entire work shows that Bruckner was still under the effect of the criticism which he had suffered at the hands of Dessoff and others with regard to his 1st Symphony. He made every effort to avoid the impetuousness and daring of the earlier work, and since he had also been accused of formlessness he now tried to make its structure and periodicity abundantly clear by inserting pauses at the ends of various sections, thereby earning the work its nickname *Pausensymphonie*. Even so the 2nd is in many respects far more 'Brucknerian' than the 1st, especially in the thematic unity which was later to become such a

Anton Bruckner and Hanslick. Silhouette by Otto Böhler

predominant feature of his work, fusing the four movements of his symphonies into a single, immense whole. Further elements which appear here for the first time and which were to become of utmost importance later on are the occurrence of the rhythmic figure of the trumpet entry (a dotted version of what has become known as 'the Bruckner rhythm'[1]), the extended length and structural importance of the *coda*, and the sudden contrasts between *pianissimo* and *fortissimo* which irresistibly remind the listener of effects in registration on the organ.

[1] The combination of duplet and triplet in the form of ♩ ♩ ♩ ♩ ♩ or ♩ ♩ ♩ ♩ ♩.

During the time he was engaged on this work one important event occurred in Bruckner's life: the first performance of his Mass in F minor, which took place under his own direction in the church of St. Augustin in Vienna on 27 June 1872. After the final rehearsal Herbeck is reported to have said to him: 'Bruckner, I only know two Masses: this one and Beethoven's *Solemnis*!', and the performance proved an enormous success with both the artistic world and the audience. Franz Liszt, whose acquaintance Bruckner had made in Pest in 1865, expressed himself very favourably about the work, and Hanslick in the *Neue Freie Presse* also praised it. Only one critic saw fit to describe the *Credo* as a 'Christian "Wolf's Glen"' (an allusion to Weber's *Freischütz*), which was the first time, and certainly not the last, that Bruckner had to endure actual invective from the press.

Bruckner's arrival in heaven. Silhouette by Otto Böhler

Whenever possible Bruckner paid short visits to his beloved Upper Austria—to Steyr, St. Florian, Kremsmünster, and to his old friends in and around Linz, particularly the von Mayfelds—but apart from these brief trips he remained in Vienna, where he gave up to forty lessons a week at St. Anna, at the Conservatorium and to his private pupils. Naturally these teaching activities improved his financial position noticeably, but they also robbed him of much valuable time which might have been spent on his own work. His energies seem to have been boundless, however, and soon after completing his 2nd Symphony he settled down to work on his Symphony No. 3 in D minor, which he later always referred to as the 'Wagner Symphony', a work which perhaps was to bring him more joy and also more grief than any other composition. This symphony occupied him throughout the year 1873 (it was completed on New Year's Eve 1873), and he even worked on it during his stay in Marienbad, where he took a cure in August. From there he went straight to Bayreuth, and in September 1873 the famous meeting with Wagner took place during which he showed him the scores of the 2nd and 3rd Symphonies.[1] Bruckner himself describes this encounter in detail,[2] how enthusiastic 'the Master' was about the D minor Symphony and with what friendship he treated him. Bruckner asked Wagner's permission to dedicate one of the two works to him, and Wagner chose the 3rd Symphony. Bruckner was overjoyed—and by the next morning had promptly forgotten which of the two works Wagner had selected! This resulted in the little note with its double autograph, on which Bruckner wrote: 'Symphony in D minor, where the trumpet begins the theme. A. Bruckner', and Wagner scribbled in reply: 'Yes! Yes! Kindest regards! Richard Wagner.' From that day onward Wagner always proclaimed himself openly as Bruckner's friend and supporter. For instance when he came to Vienna in 1875 a reception committee of admirers was awaiting him at the station, but he ignored them all and rushed over to Bruckner saying: 'When will the symphony be performed?' Then, turning to the others, he said: 'Bruckner—he is my man!' The nickname 'the Trumpet' also dates from this time, a nickname which Wagner assigned to Bruckner, and which has since been transferred to the 3rd Symphony.

On Bruckner's return to Vienna another great joy awaited him. After many efforts Herbeck had found him a sponsor in the person of Prince Johann Liechtenstein, who was prepared to finance a performance of the Symphony No. 2 in C minor. The performance took place on 26 October 1873 in the *Grosser Musikvereinssaal* with Bruckner conducting the Philharmonic Orchestra—the same orchestra which had turned the work down as 'unplayable' only a few months earlier. To Bruckner's great surprise not only the audience but also the members of the orchestra honoured him with a standing ovation, and Ludwig Speidel in the *Fremdenblatt* praised the work highly. Hanslick was somewhat more critical, but not yet as devastating as he was to become later. However, perhaps one of the most important aspects of this performance is

[1] At that time only the first three movements of the 3rd Symphony were completed in full score; the Finale had only been sketched out.

[2] See Bruckner's letter to Baron Wolzogen, 1891.

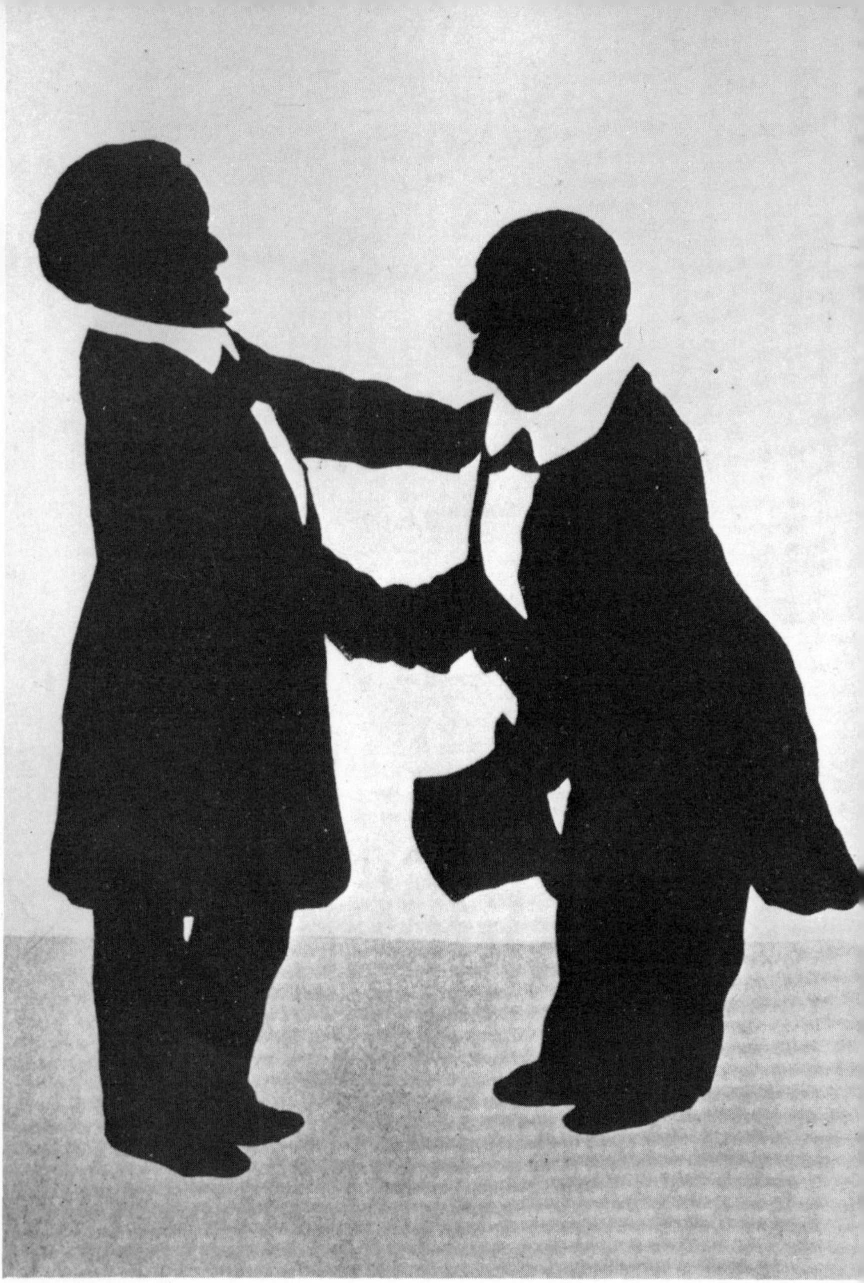

Wagner welcoming Bruckner in Bayreuth. Silhouette by Otto Böhler

Richard Wagner offering snuff to Anton Bruckner. Silhouette by Otto Böhler

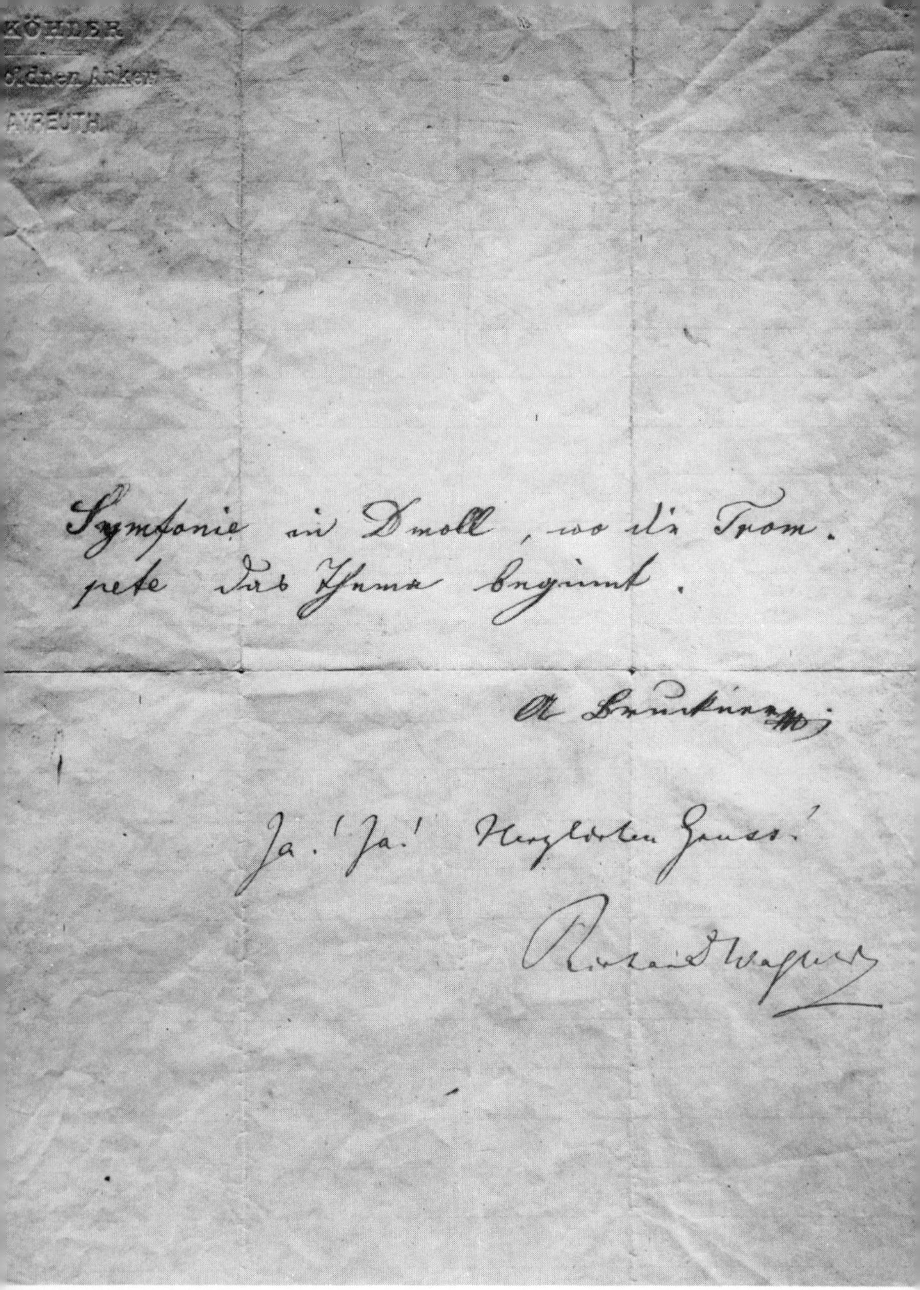

KÖHLER
Anker
AYREUTH

Symfonie in Dmoll, wo die Trompete das Thema beginnt.

A. Bruckner

Ja! Ja! Herzlichen Gruss!

Richard Wagner

The autographs of Bruckner and Wagner on a brief note referring to the dedication of Symphony No. 3

one which at the time must have seemed irrelevant: in the ranks of the violins of the Philharmonic Orchestra sat a young man by the name of Arthur Nikisch, who as the famous conductor of the *Gewandhaus* Orchestra in Leipzig was to become one of the foremost fighters for the recognition of Bruckner's genius. In 1919 he said: 'When I was playing in the orchestra in this symphony it immediately aroused in me that enthusiasm which today, after forty-six years, I still feel for it and its sisters.'

At about the same time, under the influence of his Bayreuth visit, Bruckner became a member of the *Akademischer Richard-Wagner-Verein*, and this move as well as his repeated insistence on the recognition accorded him by Wagner branded him as a 'Wagnerian' in the musical world of Vienna, thereby marking the beginning of the hostility from which he was to suffer for the rest of his life.

In order to understand the position fully it is necessary to know something of the musical situation in Vienna at the time. Brahms, who lived and worked in Vienna, was considered by Hanslick, the all-powerful critic, and the majority of the musical world of Vienna as the rightful successor of Beethoven and the Viennese classics. His antipode was Wagner (who had proclaimed that after Beethoven it was impossible to write a symphony) and with him the entire *Neudeutsche Schule*, the 'New German School', and strange as it may seem to us today it was considered impossible to admire and love both Brahms' and Wagner's music. So when Bruckner was stamped as a 'Wagnerian', he immediately became the object of musical party politics, and the entire pro-Wagner group saw its chance of improving its position by establishing Bruckner as a Wagnerian symphonist in opposition to Brahms. Not only did this tag lead to great misconceptions about Bruckner's music for many years to come, for history gives ample proof of the tenacity of such arbitrary classifications, but it also made him the target *par excellence* for the most virulent poison that ever came from Hanslick's pen. Brahms expressed himself disdainfully about Bruckner on several occasions, and it lay in the nature of the two men, the North German and the Austrian, the Protestant and the Catholic, that they found very little common ground and simply did not understand each other. This was proved conclusively when friends of the two composers tried to bring them together for a personal meeting in the *Gasthaus 'Zum roten Igel'* in 1889. The evening passed pleasantly enough, but the conversation was very superficial and the only point on which the two masters thoroughly agreed was in their liking for certain typically Austrian dishes! However, as far as the evidence goes it would appear that Brahms never participated in the active campaign against Bruckner, and dissociated himself from the vitriolic excesses of his supporters. It is true that his remarks about Bruckner's music were disparaging but, as Friedrich Blume writes in his article on Bruckner in *Die Musik in Geschichte und Gegenwart*, perhaps Brahms would not have been too pleased either had he heard Bruckner say that 'he preferred a Strauss waltz to a Brahms symphony!'

While we are on this point, the time has perhaps come to extend some measure of fairness and understanding to Hanslick and his circle. Considering

Vienna, Restaurant 'Zum roten Igel' at the Wildpretmarkt, site of the historic meeting between Brahms and Bruckner

the slow progress which Bruckner's music has made outside the German-speaking countries, is it surprising that the generation of Hanslick, rooted as they were in the idiom of the Viennese classics and their successors, simply could not take in Bruckner's gigantic symphonic utterances, or tolerate the shattering impact which these symphonies must have made upon their well-established musical concepts? There is certainly no excuse for the kind of language with which Hanslick and his follows attempted to ruin and ridicule Bruckner, but again let us be honest: was it any more 'gentlemanly' of Hugo Wolf, one of Bruckner's most ardent supporters, to write that 'one single cymbal crash by Bruckner is worth all the four symphonies of Brahms with the serenades thrown in'? In the second half of the nineteenth century the music critics were enjoying a steep and rapid climb to power, a power almost of life and death over composers and their works. Unfortunately, inflated with this newly acquired power, they sometimes lost all restraint, forgot their tact and good manners and gave free rein to their pens and their journalistic inventiveness at the cost of common decency and artistic integrity.

Meanwhile Bruckner had completed his D minor Symphony in its first version. This first version, which has never been performed, contained several direct quotations from Wagner, quotations which Bruckner deleted in later revisions. In order to obtain more free time for composing he petitioned for a regular government grant, but his petition was rejected, as was also a repetition of his 1867 application to the university of Vienna for the creation of a lectureship in musical theory; nor did his consequent attempts to find the backing for a move to England meet with any success. In the midst of these various efforts to organise his personal life, Bruckner was already at work on his next symphony, No. 4 in E flat which he called the *Romantic*. This is the only occasion on which, following the custom of the romantic movement, he officially gave a title to a symphonic work, although sometimes he referred to his symphonies by nicknames: No. 1 he always called '*das kecke Beserl*' (impossible to translate into English—perhaps 'the cheeky brat'), No. 5 he occasionally referred to as the 'Fantastic', and on several occasions he said about No. 6 '*die Sechste ist die Keckste*' ('the Sixth is the cheekiest'). Work on the E flat Symphony began late in 1873 while he was still engaged on the Finale of No. 3, and in its first version, which again has never been performed, the score was completed in November 1874. Despite Dessoff's promise to include the 'Wagner Symphony' in the programmes of the Philharmonic Orchestra, Bruckner did not hear a single performance of these last two symphonies at the time. Nevertheless, immediately after the completion of No. 4 he settled down and began the next, the gigantic Symphony No. 5 in B flat, which occupied him throughout the year 1875 and which brings to a close the first of the two great 'creative waves' mentioned earlier. The score of No. 5 was completed in November 1875. During the ensuing three years Bruckner made various minor alterations but these are not significant enough to constitute different 'versions'. Apart from the 9th Symphony which was unfinished at his death, No. 5 is the only one which Bruckner never heard performed.[1]

[1] But see also p. 87

Ferdinand Löwe (1865–1925), Bruckner's pupil and friend. Together with the brothers Schalk he was largely responsible for the revisions of the first printed editions of Bruckner's works

Franz Schalk

Vienna University

In July 1875 Bruckner, with true 'Upper Austrian stubbornness' as he himself termed it, proposed yet a third time to the university of Vienna that a lectureship in harmony and counterpoint be created, and at long last, despite Hanslick's opposition, his application was successful. Bruckner was appointed to the post, which was initially an honorary one but for which from 1877 onwards he received a fixed salary, and on 25 November 1875 he gave his opening oration. Even in old age Bruckner always remained youthful at heart, and throughout these last twenty years of his life the contact with academic youth was one of his constant joys. He called them 'my *gaudeamus*'; they were open to his new and progressive ideas, gave him their enthusiastic support and were perhaps amongst the first to realise the true genius of Bruckner and the greatness of his humanity and personality. The freshness with which he presented his subject matter and the way in which he enlivened his lectures by illustrating them with examples from the great composers both of the past and of his own day, notably Richard Wagner, assured him of an ever increasing stream of listeners. Nor was the contact between student and master confined to the university: outside the lecture room Bruckner spent many convivial hours with his favourite pupils, and for many of them attendance at dinner (which Bruckner was in the habit of taking at a late hour in one of various inns and restaurants) was virtually a command. Foremost amongst the students who were later to promote Bruckner's music so ardently were the brothers Joseph and Franz Schalk and Ferdinand Löwe.

Vienna, the house Hessgasse 7 where Bruckner lived 1877–95

An event which gave Bruckner a new incentive was a second performance of his Symphony No. 2 on 20 February 1876, which Herbeck had succeeded in arranging within the framework of the *Gesellschaftskonzerte*. This performance gave rise to the first series of revisions, for at Herbeck's suggestion Bruckner had made various changes in the score of the symphony before the performance, including some drastic cuts. By all accounts Herbeck must have made almost superhuman efforts of persuasion to convince Bruckner of the necessity of these cuts, and it will always remain a matter of conjecture to what extent these alterations were truly sanctioned by Bruckner and express his final wish. This vexatious problem of the relative authenticity of the 'versions' is one which all who concern themselves with the 'true' Bruckner are continually coming across. The success of the performance, which Bruckner conducted, was mixed: the audience appears to have applauded it enthusiastically, but in the press an increasing acerbity was noticeable, and one critic went so far as to call Bruckner 'a fool and a half'.

The main events in Bruckner's personal life during the next three years, from the beginning of 1876 until December 1878, were a visit to Bayreuth in August 1876 for the first performance of the *Ring des Nibelungen*, an occasion on which he renewed his close friendship with Wagner, visits to St. Florian and Upper Austria, and the move from his home in the Währingerstrasse to a flat on the fourth floor of a house in the Hessgasse. This house belonged to one of Bruckner's admirers, Dr. Anton Ölzelt-Newin, whom Bruckner had first

#4

met on one of his visits to Klosterneuburg and who now showed his admiration in a concrete form by allowing Bruckner to live there rent free. The flat was spacious and had a beautiful view, but its furnishings were more than sparse and provided striking evidence of Bruckner's singularity of purpose. His bedroom contained his bed and nothing else, and the other room was occupied by his piano, his harmonium, a chest of drawers, an armchair and his working table; the only other objects being the laurel wreaths which he had received on various occasions and which were hung on the walls of the hall, and stacks of music and manuscript paper on the piano, on the chest of drawers and on the floor of both rooms! Last but not least, on 24 January 1878 he was appointed a full member of the *Hofkapelle*, to which he had been attached in an unpaid capacity *in Exspektanz* for the last ten years, and this increased his annual income by 800 guilders—a most necessary increase, for when he had completed his Symphony No. 4 in 1874, his financial position was such that he could not even afford to have the score copied.

Musically these three years were devoted almost entirely to revision, beginning with the Symphony No. 2. The year 1876 also saw minor alterations in his Masses in D minor and F minor. Then in 1876–77 followed a thorough revision of Symphony No. 3 which, according to Bruckner's letter to von Mayfeld, he had already 'considerably improved' in 1874. This revision resulted in the second version, from which all Wagner quotations had been eliminated and in which the symphony had its first performance in December 1877. Bruckner also did some minor revision to the 1st and 2nd Symphonies in 1877, and in 1878 he began a thorough revision of No. 4 which eventually resulted in the second version of 1878–80. The first, second and fourth movements were considerably revised in 1878, and at the same time he composed an entirely new Scherzo, the one now generally known as the 'Hunting Scherzo'. In this initial revision, however, the Finale was basically unchanged, and despite certain alterations the second version of the Finale still corresponded to the first version, which Bruckner called the *Volksfest*, a comparatively lighthearted and unproblematical movement which probably owes its name to the annual festival in Wels. Throughout this period (1876–78) he was also at work on his 5th Symphony in the score of which, as has already been mentioned, he made only minor adjustments and alterations, the most important of which is the addition of a bass tuba part. During 1878–79, overlapping the beginning of the second 'creative wave', he again revised his 2nd Symphony, which now attained its second and final version, and in 1879–80 he put the finishing touches to the 4th Symphony, adding the new and more dramatic Finale. It is thus the first and second movements of the 1878 revision together with the 'Hunting Scherzo' of 1878 and the Finale of 1879–80 which constitute the second version of the 4th Symphony. It is in this form that Bruckner bequeathed it to the *Hofbibliothek* (although he still made some minor changes in 1881 and about 1886), and this second version is the one usually performed nowadays.

The darkest day of Bruckner's entire musical life falls within that period: 16 December 1877. This was the day on which Herbeck, having overcome

Anton Bruckner in his home (1894?)

very strong opposition, was to conduct the Symphony No. 3 in D minor, the 'Wagner Symphony', in one of the *Gesellschaftskonzerte*, but on 28 October Herbeck suddenly died, and Bruckner lost one of his staunchest personal friends and supporters. Through the efforts of August Göllerich,[1] a member of the Chamber of Deputies, the work was retained on the programme, but Bruckner had to conduct it himself. For one thing the novelty of conception and invention of the work must have bewildered his listeners, and for another Bruckner's abilities as an orchestral conductor quite clearly were not such that he could convince an audience through his interpretative powers. In short, the performance was a catastrophe, with the audience leaving the hall in ever-increasing numbers and the members of the orchestra fleeing from the rostrum the moment the last note was played. Only a handful of listeners remained to the end, mainly Bruckner's pupils, who gave him a standing ovation in a futile effort to cheer him up. Bruckner refused to be consoled and kept saying: 'Leave me alone—nobody wants me!'

And then the miracle happened. Despite the fiasco which he had just witnessed the publisher Theodor Rättig approached Bruckner and offered to publish the symphony. At first Bruckner could not believe his ears, but Rättig meant what he said, and in 1878 Bussjäger & Rättig issued the 'Wagner Symphony' in its second version in score, parts, and a reduction for piano duet prepared by Gustav Mahler and Rudolf Krzyzanowsky, thereby becoming the first to publish a Bruckner symphony. For the first time also Hanslick, infuriated both by Bruckner's avowed admiration of Wagner and by his success with his students, attacked the symphony with his most biting irony, saying that it appeared to him as a 'vision of Beethoven's Ninth coming to friendly terms with Wagner's *Walküre* and ending up by being crushed under the horses' hooves'.

As a result of the disastrous performance of the 3rd Symphony and with his time so completely taken up with his teaching activities and revision work, few new compositions came from Bruckner's pen during these three years. Besides some minor works for male chorus, the only important composition of that period is the Motet *Tota pulchra es* (1878) for tenor solo, mixed chorus and organ, which Bruckner wrote for the silver jubilee of his friend and protector Bishop Rudigier of Linz, and which ranks amongst the half dozen or so of his finest small-scale liturgical works.

In December 1878, despite the failure of his efforts to obtain performances of his works in Berlin, the second of Bruckner's great 'creative waves' began with the composition of his String Quintet in F, his only chamber music work apart from the early String Quartet of 1862, which was more in the nature of an exercise based on his studies with Kitzler. The work owed its origin to an episode which had occurred well over seventeen years earlier, when Hellmesberger, one of the examiners in the *Piaristenkirche*, had asked Bruckner after the examination whether he would like to write a work for him and

[1] Father of August Göllerich jun. who was Bruckner's pupil at the time and later became his official biographer.

his string quartet. The score of the Quintet was completed in June 1879. At Hellmesberger's request he replaced the Scherzo, which Hellmesberger considered too difficult, by an Intermezzo composed in December 1879, but eventually the original Scherzo was retained. This Quintet has often been called a 'symphony in disguise', but nothing could be further from the truth. It is in fact amazing how perfectly Bruckner the symphonist adapted himself to the world of chamber music, considering that for decades he had only been concerned with large choral or orchestral forces. If anything the Quintet stands in direct line of succession to the late string quartets of Beethoven. During June 1879 Bruckner composed another of his deeply moving motets, *Os justi*, which he was to hear sung in August of that year in St. Florian, and Auer also places the composition of the second[1] *Christus factus est* in that period.

It is as if these works of 1879 were a gathering of forces before Bruckner could again take the deep breath necessary for the mighty sweep of a symphony, and in September of that year he began the first movement of his Symphony No. 6 in A. Work on this symphony, however, was interrupted by the final revision of No. 4. This revision was completed on 5 June 1880, the eve of yet another memorable performance: the Mass in D minor which, with the *Locus iste* inserted as the gradual and the *Os justi* as the offertory, was the first work of Bruckner's to be heard in Vienna since the calamitous first performance of the 3rd Symphony in 1877. It was thirteen years since the Mass had last been heard in Vienna, and it was at Hellmesberger's instigation that the performance took place, the same Hellmesberger who did not dare to perform the String Quintet for fear of offending Hanslick and the press. Again the work had a deeply moving effect on all listeners, and Hellmesberger expressed his great admiration to Bruckner. After this happy event Bruckner took one of his few long holidays, and for once he travelled fairly extensively. After a week in St. Florian he visited Oberammergau where he saw the Passion Play and then went via Munich to Switzerland where he revelled in the beauty of the landscape. During his trip he also played the cathedral organs in Geneva, Freiburg, Bern, Zürich and Lucerne. He ended his holiday where he started—at St. Florian.

After his return to Vienna an ailment in his feet and legs, from which later he was to suffer considerably, first made itself noticeable, and a further disappointment awaited him when he heard that the position of Assistant Conductor of the *Wiener Männergesangsverein* for which he had applied had been filled by another musician, though it must be said that in later years this choir did much for Bruckner by performing his works. In spite of these adversities Bruckner now concentrated his energies on his 6th Symphony, which he had begun almost a year earlier, and the score of the entire work was finished in St. Florian in September 1881. With it Bruckner completed what is perhaps the most closely-knit of all his symphonies. Set in the 'bright' key of A it stands in contrast to all its predecessors in tonal colouring, and it is one of the incomprehensible vagaries of interpreters and listeners alike that this work should always have been (and still is to some extent) less frequently performed in

[1] See footnote on p. 28.

The Stiftskirche *of St. Florian, seen from the monastery farm*

Vienna, Gesellschaft der Musikfreunde

public than any of the others. One reason for this neglect may lie in the rhythmic intricacies of the first movement, for here the 'Bruckner rhythm', which has been mentioned in connection with the 2nd Symphony and which gained such ascendancy particularly in the 3rd and 4th Symphonies, occurs in a vertical combination as well as horizontally, and this is apt to make for some difficulty both in performance and in listening. Bruckner himself heard the complete work only once, in a rehearsal of the Philharmonic Orchestra under Jahn in which 'novelties' were tried out; in public performance only the two middle movements were played during his lifetime.

Bruckner was now in his fifty-seventh year, and at long last the tide seemed to be turning in his favour. In February 1881 Hans Richter and the Philharmonic Orchestra gave the first performance of the 'Romantic' Symphony, No. 4. It was after rehearsal for this performance that an event occurred which Richter could not forget for the rest of his days. At the end of the rehearsal Bruckner, beaming with happiness, came up to him and pressed a *Taler* into his hand, saying: 'Take this and drink my health with a glass of beer!', a moving testimonial to Bruckner's warm-hearted naïvety. The performance proved a triumph for Bruckner and even the hostile sections of the Viennese press could not but give him his due, including the *Neue Freie Presse* which spoke of an 'unusual success'. Other papers, however, were eulogistic in their praise, and the *Wiener Abendpost* stated plainly that Bruckner must be counted amongst Austria's greatest composers. But one of the most important comments and one which reveals true insight into Bruckner came from Eduard Kremser in *Das Vaterland*. He wrote: 'Bruckner is a follower of Wagner only in the sense in which Wagner is a follower of Beethoven and Beethoven of Mozart.' It might perhaps be mentioned in this connection that, pressed by his friends who adhered to the 'New German School' and considered it essential that all music should have a 'programme', Bruckner tried to put the 'contents' of the symphony into words. It is a feeble attempt at romantic description including 'Dawn', 'Horsemen sallying forth', 'shadowy forests' and the rest of the romantic trimmings. The only movement to which some sort of programme could perhaps be ascribed is the 'Hunt' of the Scherzo with the ensuing Trio, which in one of the manuscripts bears the title 'Dance tune while the hunters are resting'. Several years later, on 27 January 1891, Bruckner made an equally feeble attempt at 'explaining' his 8th Symphony to Felix Weingartner in a letter, but his true attitude towards such programmatic explanations was shown when, on the occasion of a performance of the 7th Symphony in Vienna, Joseph Schalk wrote a lengthy 'programme' as an introduction to the work. Viktor Hruby reports Bruckner as having said: 'If he has to write poetry, why does he have to pick on my symphony?', and this is surely much more in keeping with Bruckner's personality and music.

As if to give thanks to his Creator for this great success, Bruckner sketched out a *Te Deum* in May 1881, but this first version was to remain a fragment, and the work was eventually completed in its second version in 1884. The *Te Deum* was put aside in order to continue work on the 6th Symphony, and at its completion Bruckner had high hopes that Hellmesberger would perform his String Quintet during the 1881–82 concert season. But once again Hellmesberger lacked the courage to come out into the open in support of Bruckner, though he had expressed his great admiration of the work in private. It was left to Franz Schalk and a small group of ardent disciples to give the first performance of Bruckner's great chamber music work (omitting the Finale) in a private concert of the *Akademischer Richard-Wagner-Verein* in November 1881 in the *Bösendorfer-Saal*. The concert being held in private, the press made no mention of it, but Bruckner expressed himself highly satisfied. In December 1881 Bruckner's former pupil Felix Mottl, who had meanwhile become conductor in Karlsruhe, performed the 4th Symphony there, but the work met with no success. However, it proved possible to keep the news of this latest defeat from Bruckner. The year 1881 also saw performances of various choral compositions, and in April 1882 his F minor Mass was finally performed in the *Hofkapelle* for which it was originally intended.

In 1877 Johannes Brahms had received an honorary doctorate of the University of Cambridge, and this as well as the fact that Bruckner moved a great deal in academic circles may have led him to make an application to the same university to be granted a doctorate. A few years later, in 1886, he addressed similar petitions to the universities of Philadelphia and Cincinnati, but all these efforts were of no avail. This great honour, which meant so much to him, was finally bestowed on him by the University of Vienna in 1891.

The ink, so to speak, was still wet on the final pages of his 6th Symphony when Bruckner, as was his custom, began work on Symphony No 7 in E, which was to occupy him to the exclusion of almost everything else for two years, from September 1881 until September 1883. Only two other minor compositions fall into that period, one of them the *Ave Maria* for contralto with organ accompaniment which owes its existence to the fact that once again Bruckner had lost his heart to a girl, this time one with a particularly beautiful voice. The other great event of 1882 was another visit to Bayreuth, this time to be present at the first performance of *Parsifal*. This was the last time that Bruckner was to be together with his beloved 'Master', and Wagner is reported to have said of him at that time: 'I only know one composer who measures up to Beethoven, and that is Bruckner.' During this visit Wagner is also reputed to have promised Bruckner that he would perform all his works. Whether the promise was meant seriously or not is a matter for conjecture, but in any case Wagner's death on 13 February 1883 brought it to nothing.

On the way back to Vienna Bruckner spent some time at St. Florian, where he composed the Scherzo and virtually completed the first movement of his 7th Symphony, and he also paid visits to Wilhering, Kremsmünster and Steyr. Back in Vienna work on the symphony continued, and it was then that Bruckner heard his entire 6th Symphony in rehearsal under Jahn. Although the orchestra was enthusiastic about the work, Jahn did not dare to include the whole symphony in one of his programmes and only performed the two middle movements in public in February 1883. It is perhaps of interest to mention the report of one of Bruckner's pupils, Lamberg, who said that after the performance there was a colossal ovation, and whereas 'Hanslick sat there, frigid and immobile like a sphinx, Brahms joined in the general applause', proof again that Brahms was by no means as implacably hostile towards Bruckner as is so often made out. Apart from this performance of the two middle movements of the 6th Symphony, Vienna heard the String Quintet on two occasions in 1883, a further performance of the Mass in F minor (June 1883) and a performance on two pianos by Joseph Schalk and Ferdinand Löwe of the 3rd Symphony (May 1883). This, incidentally, was not an isolated instance: as Löwe and Schalk did not have the necessary means and influence to promote orchestral performances of Bruckner's works, they took the only course open to them and brought them before the public by playing them on two pianos.

On 22 January 1883, three weeks before Wagner's death, Bruckner began the Adagio of his 7th Symphony, perhaps the greatest of all his Adagios. In a letter to Felix Mottl he wrote: 'One day I came home and felt very sad. The thought had crossed my mind that before long the Master would die, and then the C sharp minor theme of the Adagio came to me.' It is interesting to note that in this movement Bruckner makes his first use of the quartet of Wagner tubas, and the news of Wagner's death came to him when the composition had progressed as far as the great climax (letter W in the score) which is underlined by the famous cymbal clash about which there has been so much argument. This great climax is ushered in by sequential treatment of a theme which Bruckner also used in his *Te Deum* to the words 'Non confundar in aeternum', words which have such prophetic implication for both Wagner's and his own music. Understandably the news of Wagner's death was a shattering blow to Bruckner, and it found its artistic sublimation in the beginning of the *coda* of the Adagio, that sombre and overwhelming passage for tubas and horns which Bruckner always referred to as the 'funeral music for the Master'. There remained the Finale which Bruckner wrote during the summer of 1883 and completed at St. Florian in August of that year, after he had paid another short visit to Wagner's grave at Bayreuth. In September the score of the 7th Symphony was completed, the symphony which was to bring him the greatest joy, the fullest measure of success, and which was at long last to establish his reputation on an international level.

Elated by the completion of his 7th Symphony, Bruckner turned back to the *Te Deum*, which he had sketched out in its first version in 1881, and completed the second version between September 1883 and March 1884. Written for solo quartet, chorus and orchestra with organ, it is his mightiest hymn of praise to the Almighty and is considered by many to be his greatest sacred composition. It is certainly his most powerful, and its contrasts, when the music dies away to nothing, and then re-enters *fortissimo* in chorus, orchestra and on the *pleno* of the organ, make an indescribable impression on the listener, filling him with awe and reverence and awakening in him a realisation of human insignificance. The crowning glory of the work is its last movement, where the theme from the Adagio of the 7th Symphony ushers in the greatest climax imaginable, when the words 'Non confundar in aeternum' are contrapuntally interwoven with 'In te, Domine, speravi' and the whole work thunders to its victorious C major conclusion. The opening string figure of the *Te Deum* was to recur again in Bruckner's music, written in the shaky handwriting of his last years: it appears in the sketches of the unfinished Finale of his 9th Symphony. Hellmesberger, when he had seen the score of the *Te Deum*, suggested that Bruckner should dedicate it to the Emperor, but Bruckner said it was no longer free. He had already dedicated it to 'his dear Lord.'

After a visit to Prague he composed the third and finest setting of the Motet *Christus factus est*, and on his return to Vienna he met Franz Liszt again and asked if he might dedicate his 2nd Symphony to him. Liszt promised to have a thorough look at the work, but after his departure Bruckner discovered that Liszt had left the score behind in the *Schottenhof* where he had been staying. This hurt Bruckner most deeply, and when the symphony came to be printed he omitted the dedication. It is understandable that there could be little contact between the suave, worldly 'Abbé' Liszt and Bruckner, but again due credit must be given: after Liszt had heard the Adagio of the 7th Symphony under Mottl in Karlsruhe in 1885 he spared no effort to promote and further Bruckner's work.

In 1884 Bruckner paid his by now customary visits to Bayreuth, Munich, Kremsmünster and St. Florian, and his sixtieth birthday was spent in Vöcklabruck where he had been staying for some time with his sister Rosalie. But the 4 September 1884 was a birthday in a second sense, for it saw the completion of the sketch of the first movement of his 8th Symphony on which he had been working for some time. The composition of this, his last complete symphony, was to engage Bruckner from the late summer of 1884 until July 1887, and it will be dealt with in detail at a later stage. Although every fibre of Bruckner's being must have been involved in the creation of this monumental symphony, he still found time to compose a short *Präludium* for harmonium, an *a capella Salvum fac populum tuum* for Klosterneuburg, and the great *Ecce sacerdos* for mixed chorus, three trombones and organ.

Apart from the composition of the 8th Symphony, however, the years 1884–85 were dominated mainly by performances and publications, the String Quintet being the first Bruckner work to be published (by Albert Gutmann in 1884) since Rättig had printed the 3rd Symphony in 1878. In April 1884 the Quintet had again been performed in Vienna in a concert of the *Akademischer Gesangsverein*. The second half of 1884 was an anxious time for Bruckner. Arthur Nikisch, the conductor of the *Gewandhaus* Orchestra in Leipzig, had accepted the 7th Symphony for performance, and the date scheduled was 27 June 1884, but unexpected circumstances and the opposition of an anti-Bruckner faction necessitated two postponements, so that the first performance was not in fact given until 30 December. Bruckner was present on this great occasion, and although reports about the reception of the symphony on the part of the audience are contradictory, there can be no doubt about the over-

Arthur Nikisch (1855–1922) conductor of the Leipzig Gewandhaus Orchestra

Anton Bruckner as one of the disciples in Fritz von Uhde's painting 'The last Supper' (1885–86)

whelming, unprecedented acclaim which it was accorded by all the press. A great deal of the credit for this success must undoubtedly go to Nikisch. His greatness as a conductor must have ensured a truly memorable interpretation, and he had also taken the trouble of inviting the Leipzig music critics to his home before the performance in order to introduce them to the music at the piano. Thus the 30 December 1884 marks one of the greatest turning points in Bruckner's life. He was now firmly established in Germany as well as internationally, and this position was further consolidated by the second German performance of the 7th Symphony on 10 March 1885 in Munich under Hermann Levi, the first conductor of *Parsifal*, whom Bruckner referred to as 'my artistic father' ever after. The performance, which took place only after Levi had overcome a certain measure of opposition in his own orchestra, was the greatest triumph which Bruckner had hitherto witnessed, and all the critics present vied with each other in heaping praise on the work. King Ludwig II of Bavaria accepted the dedication of the symphony, which enhanced its reputation still further, and Bruckner's breakthrough as a composer of the highest order was now an established fact in all musical circles—except certain groups in Vienna. While in Leipzig Bruckner had made several unsuccessful attempts to get his 7th Symphony published, but now Albert Gutmann showed himself ready to undertake the publication, though he demanded 1000 guilders towards the costs. It was Levi who undertook to collect the necessary sum, and under the supervision of Joseph Schalk score and parts were issued in 1885.

During the last eleven years of his life Bruckner at last began to reap the fruit of his lifelong labours. His name became internationally known, and his music was heard throughout Europe and America as the following list of performances of his symphonies clearly shows[1]:

1885 No. 3: Dresden, Frankfurt, The Hague (2), Utrecht, New York
No. 7: Munich, Karlsruhe
1886 No. 3: Linz, The Hague
No. 4: Sondershausen
No. 7: Vienna, Graz, Hamburg, Cologne, Amsterdam, New York, Boston, Chicago
1887 No. 7: Berlin, Dresden (2), Cologne, London (2), Budapest
1888 No. 4: Vienna, New York
No. 7: Graz (2)
1889 No. 7: Vienna
1890 No. 3: Vienna, Linz, Salzburg
No. 4: Munich
1891 No. 1: Vienna
No. 3: Vienna, Prague, Nürnberg, London
No. 4: Graz, Nürnberg
No. 7: Berlin

[1] From Gerh. F. Wehle, *Anton Bruckner im Spiegel seiner Zeitgenossen*, G. E. Schroeder-Verlag, Garmisch-Partenkirchen, 1964.

Klosterneuburg, Emperor's Wing

Three great Bruckner conductors: Hermann Levi (left), Hans Richter (right), Felix Mottl (centre, standing

1892 No. 3: Vienna, Amsterdam
No. 4: Vienna
No. 8: Vienna
1893 No. 3: Berlin, Munich, Heidelberg
No. 4: Brünn (Brno), Troppau
No. 7: Munich, Leipzig, Hamburg, Breslau
No. 8: Olnütz (Olomouc)
1894 No. 2: Vienna (2)
No. 3: Paris
No. 5: Graz
No. 7: Berlin, Dresden
1895 No. 2: Graz, Munich
No. 4: Linz, Berlin, Hamburg, Dresden
No. 5: Budapest
No. 7: Frankfurt
No. 8: Dresden
1896 No. 1: Graz
No. 4: Vienna, Linz, England (?)
No. 7: Vienna, Troppau, Stuttgart

Various honours were bestowed on him, the Austrian Emperor decorated him with the Order of Franz-Joseph (which was coupled with a grant from the Emperor's private purse) in 1886, and the Honorary Doctorate from the University of Vienna was to follow in 1891. Kaulbach painted his portrait, and Fritz von Uhde incorporated Bruckner as one of the twelve disciples in his monumental 'Last Supper', an honour which made a particularly deep impression on him. Financially things also took a turn for the better during his last years. From 1889 onwards he received a regular grant from a group of Austrian industrialists, from 1890 onwards one from the Austrian government, and in the matter of publications he was further assisted by his pupil Friedrich Eckstein, who financed the publication of the *Te Deum*, Hermann Levi, who made another collection towards the printing of the 4th Symphony, and the Emperor himself, who gave the financial support necessary for the publication of the 3rd Symphony in its third version and of the 8th Symphony. Bruckner himself received only one publisher's fee in his whole lifetime—the sum of 50 guilders from Rättig for the *Te Deum*.

At about this time another young man took his place in the ranks of Bruckner's ardent admirers and friends, a young man whose name was also to become famous and who was to achieve such greatness in the realm of the *Lied*: Hugo Wolf. Whereas the Schalk brothers and Löwe supported their beloved teacher by trying to bring his music to the fore, Wolf fought for Bruckner in a journalistic capacity. Many are the articles he wrote about Bruckner and his music although, as has already been said, at times he went too far in his youthful enthusiasm and descended to an aggressive style unworthy of Bruckner as well

View overlooking Klosterneuburg, near Vienna

as of himself. Bruckner, for his part, was a great admirer of Wolf's work, and apart from a short period of estrangement caused by some minor friction, the friendship between the two composers lasted until Bruckner's death.

During the years 1885–87 Bruckner's life was marked outwardly by intensive work as a teacher and lecturer, so that comparatively little time was left for his compositions. What little time there was he spent on his 8th Symphony. Only two shorter compositions date from this period, the ineffably beautiful *a capella* Motet *Virga Jesse* of September 1885 and *Um Mitternacht* for male chorus and tenor solo of February 1886. It was mainly during his holidays that Bruckner could settle down to concentrated work, for during the academic year his time was too short and was interrupted by minor journeys in connection with performances of his works. Every summer saw him in Steyr and St. Florian, from where he frequently visited Kremsmünster, and usually he also spent Christmas at St. Florian. It was at Steyr in 1885 that he completed the first draft of the 8th Symphony, and again at Steyr in September 1887 that he finally finished the score of that symphony in its first version. Although performances abroad were increasing rapidly in number, Vienna continued to ignore him, and when the Philharmonic Orchestra did consider performing his 7th Symphony in Vienna during the 1885–86 concert season, Bruckner asked them not to do so, giving as his reason that 'the Vienna press might have a detrimental effect on his recent successes in Germany'. So great was Bruckner's fear of Hanslick! In 1885 the only two Austrian performances worth noting in this context are the first performance of the *Te Deum* in Vienna in May, which Bruckner himself conducted and in which the orchestra was replaced by two pianos, and a further performance of his E minor Mass in Linz in October. One minor event, which took place in November 1885, also bears mention. On the Feast of St. Leopold, the patron saint of Austria, there was a special celebration in Klosterneuburg which on this occasion the Emperor attended in person. As he entered the church, a mighty improvisation on the *Kaiserlied*, the Emperor's Hymn, burst forth from the great organ. It is said that the Emperor stood still for a moment, looked upwards and murmured: 'Ah, Bruckner!'

1885 also marks the beginning of that illness which was to handicap Bruckner for the rest of his life. Presumably owing to some weakness of the heart, a form of dropsy began to set in which resulted in liquid gathering in his feet and legs which greatly hampered him in his movements and particularly in his organ playing. Later a debility of the throat was added to this illness, but it was not until the last few years of his life that these effects became severely noticeable.

During the following year, 1886, Bruckner enjoyed a good deal of success abroad, particularly with the performance of the *Te Deum* under Levi in Munich in April, at which he was personally present, and its first Viennese performance under Hans Richter in January. The success of the latter performance was such that even Hanslick had to make some positive concessions, but two months later, when Richer gave the first Viennese performance of the 7th Symphony (Karl Muck in Graz had beaten Vienna to the first Austrian performance by a matter of seven days), he once more gave his journalistic viciousness full rein and described the music as 'unnatural, bloated, contaminated and decadent'. Despite the great acclaim which the symphony had been accorded by the audience (after each movement Bruckner had been called out several times) all Hanslick's followers chimed in with him, which proves how right Bruckner had been in requesting the orchestra to leave the work unperformed for the time being.

August 1886 saw Bruckner back in Bayreuth for the first performance of *Tristan und Isolde* in the *Festspielhaus*. He spent some time with Cosima Wagner, but Liszt, whom he had also hoped to meet there again, had died just before his arrival, so that Bruckner could only pay his last respects to the man who in the last years of his life had been so active on his behalf by escorting him to the grave with a mighty organ improvisation on themes from *Parsifal*.

The year 1887 brought Bruckner some isolated performances in Austria. In April Joseph Schalk and F. Zottmann played his 5th Symphony for the first time in Vienna in a version for two pianos, and in September the *Te Deum* was performed in the new cathedral in Linz on the occasion of the consecration of the organ. More important, however, that year marked the completion of

Kremsmünster

The Brucknerstiege *in Steyr, leading to where the organist Franz Bayer lived*

the 8th Symphony and also brought forth the first sketches for the 9th.

It is now time to revert to 1884 and to trace the whole process of composition of the Symphony No. 8 in C minor, the last symphony which it was given to Bruckner to complete and the one which was to cause him so much grief.

The first sketch of the first movement was completed in Vöcklabruck on his sixtieth birthday, 4 September 1884, and by February 1885 the great Adagio had been sketched out. The symphony was completed in its first draft during his summer holidays in Steyr, on 25 August 1885, and a few days later, on 28 August, the Feast of St. Agustine, the patron saint of St. Florian, he first presented motives from the new symphony to the public in a grandiose organ improvisation in the *Stiftskirche* of St. Florian, interweaving these motives with themes from Wagner's *Götterdämmerung*. Bruckner's elation when he completed the huge Finale with the crowning glory of its *coda* where all four main themes of the symphony are piled on top of each other—a contrapuntal masterpiece which, however, is entirely natural and organic, without the slightest touch of academic artificiality—is shown by his signature on the score: 'Steyr, Stadtpfarrhof, 16 August 1885. A. Bruckner. Hallelujah!' Yet Bruckner was not so easily satisfied. For two whole years he revised, altered, corrected and polished his score, so that it was only finally completed in July 1887, and on 4 September, having had a clean copy made of the score, he sent it to Hermann Levi with the words: 'Hallelujah! At long last the Eighth is finished, and my artistic father must be the first to know about it', ending his letter with 'May it find grace!' Unfortunately Levi, one of Bruckner's greatest friends and supporters, who had moved heaven and earth to give performances of the 7th Symphony and of the *Te Deum*, just could not take in the enormous span of this new work. Knowing how much a rejection would hurt Bruckner he did not dare to write to him personally but made the facts known to him through Joseph Schalk. This was without doubt the greatest blow in Bruckner's life, greater even than the *débacle* of the first performance of the 3rd Symphony in 1877, for meanwhile he had acquired international standing and thought that he was now firmly established. This verdict from his 'artistic father' who, he knew well, acted without any trace of malice or hostility, shook his self-confidence to the roots and shattered his belief in himself as a composer. It was in consequence of this rejection that Bruckner began his second period of revisions, which was to last until 1891.

It must be made quite clear at this point that there is a vital difference between this period of revisions and the earlier one of 1876–79. In that first period it was Bruckner's own volition, the inner urge of the perfectionist, which caused him to go through his works one by one, altering, improving, amending.[1] Now, however, he was pressed and cajoled into a new series of revisions which have their origin not in Bruckner himself, but in the incomprehension with which his work was received by even his most ardent admirers and his most intimate friends. It is for this reason that the musical world is now faced with

[1] Although this statement is basically correct, it must also be remembered that in the case of the revision of Symphony No. 2 Herbeck was the motive force. Cf. p. 71.

Steyr, Stadtpfarrkirche

the virtually insoluble problem: to what extent do these alterations of the years 1887–91 really represent Bruckner's own will, and how many of them are due to pressure of some kind, to the wish to please his friends, or to obtain further performances? Due to the indefatigable efforts of the International Bruckner Society and the tremendous research work done by its editors, first Robert Haas and now Leopold Nowak, we are immeasurably nearer to the truth than anyone would ever have thought possible. At the same time a second point must be clarified and stressed. Many of the alterations which were made in the course of these revisions were made at the insistence of friends, above all of the Schalk brothers and Ferdinand Löwe, and in some cases were even made by them themselves and later sanctioned by Bruckner. Since Bruckner's original versions have come before the public, through the efforts of the International Bruckner Society and the *Musikwissenschaftlicher Verlag*, these faithful disciples of Bruckner's have suffered violent attacks which have at times bordered on defamation. It is true, of course, that in the light of our present-day knowledge and understanding of Bruckner's music many of these revisions, alterations and particularly cuts appear as distortions and mutilations which go against the very grain of Bruckner's conceptions, but it must be realised that, ill-advised as these alterations have been, they were made or suggested by Bruckner's friends from the purest motives as part of their unrelenting effort to promote his work. Bruckner was a genius. It is not surprising that those musicians, who were undoubtedly good but not of Bruckner's outstanding calibre, were influenced by the trends of their time, by conventions, and by the accepted dictum that Bruckner was a 'Wagnerian', and that therefore his orchestration had to be 'smoothed out' to conform to this concept. They did not and could not possess Bruckner's own far-reaching vision, and for this reason Bruckner let them be and said on more than one occasion that his original versions were 'for later times'. As if to set a seal on this statement, Bruckner in his last will and testament bequeathed his own scores of all his important works to the *Hofbibliothek* in Vienna (now the *Österreichische Nationalbibliothek*). It is these scores that represent his musical will, and they constitute the basis for the Complete Edition as published by the International Bruckner Society.

The first work to undergo revision at this time was the Symphony No. 4 in E flat, the 'Romantic'. Albert Gutmann had expressed his willingness to publish the symphony, demanding however the sum of 1000 guilders towards the cost. Again it was Levi who raised the funds by a collection, and eventually the work appeared in print in 1890. Most of the revision work was done by Ferdinand Löwe, who took many liberties with the score and made several major cuts which had a devasting effect on the formal structure of the work. Bruckner afterwards went through this score personally and made some further alterations of his own, and in this context two points are significant. Throughout his life Bruckner made an invariable custom of dating and either signing or initialling all important scores, thereby giving the mark of his personal authority. In the case of this version of the 4th Symphony, however,

Anton Bruckner in his sixties (about 1890)

he refrained from doing so, which Leopold Nowak quite rightly interprets as a withholding of his sanction. Secondly, Bruckner, when sending the score to Gutmann for engraving, wrote a covering letter in which he particularly requested that the symphony be printed in full in score, parts and piano reduction, and that the cuts should merely be indicated by the optional *vi-de*.[1] His request was ignored, the work was printed in the cut form, and it is in this version that it had its highly successful performance in Vienna under Hans Richter in January 1888.

Bruckner's friends now urged him to undertake a similar revision of his Symphony No. 3 in D minor, the 'Wagner Symphony', and again he bowed to their insistence. Several years earlier those same friends had already tried to persuade Bruckner to revise and shorten the work, and in fact he had begun to do so and Rättig had had fifty-two pages of the score re-engraved. Then Gustav Mahler convinced Bruckner that this revision was completely superfluous, Bruckner withdrew it, and Rättig had to scrap the plates. Now, however, the advice of his friends prevailed, and in the summer of 1888, during his holidays at St. Florian, Bruckner set to work on the symphony. The revision was completed by March 1889. This third version varies considerably from the second version of 1877, especially in the Finale where a large cut removes the first subject from the recapitulation, and it was with these cuts and alterations that the symphony was again published by Theodor Rättig in 1890, the Emperor contributing to the costs. As in this instance there can be no doubt whatsoever that all the alterations were made by Bruckner's own hand, these two versions of 1877 and 1889 present a great problem. Apparently the third version of 1889 represents the final expression of Bruckner's own will, yet it is known that a certain amount of pressure was brought to bear on him to produce this third version. The whole complex problem is set out in great detail in the preface of Fritz Oeser's edition of the score of the second version of 1877.[2] Suffice it to say here that the second and third versions stand side by side with equal justification.

Although shortly after Levi's rejection of the 8th Symphony in the autumn of 1887 Bruckner had begun the revision of the first movement this was put aside in favour of the work on the 3rd Symphony. Possibly the hurt he had received was of too recent a nature, and the wound had to be given time to heal. It was not until April 1889 that he went through the score bar by bar, and up until March 1890 it occupied him continuously. In this score the alterations are of a most far-reaching nature. The entire orchestration underwent many changes, and whereas the first version was for double woodwind only, this was now increased to triple woodwind. He also made several cuts. The most noticeable alteration occurs in the ending of the first movement which, in the

[1] This is also borne out by Bruckner's letter to Felix Weingartner of 21 March 1891 from St. Florian, in which he wrote: '. . . but please do not alter the score. It is also my most insistent request that the orchestral parts remain unaltered when they go to print. . . .'

[2] *Brucknerverlag* 1950.

Anton Bruckner at his piano (1894?)

first version, culminated in a blaze of orchestral sound, whereas in the second version it dies away *pianissimo*—the only instance in Bruckner's entire symphonic output where one of the great outer movements comes to a soft ending. In the Adagio the great climax, which originally culminated on C, now comes to its apex on E flat, and in the Trio of the Scherzo he also made vital changes and added a harp to the previous orchestration. The first performance of the 8th Symphony (in its second version—the first version remained unperformed until 1954) took place in Vienna under Hans Richter on 18 December 1892, and the ovation which Bruckner received surpassed his most optimistic expectations. At last the symphony which had brought him such bitter disappointment had been gloriously vindicated. It was published by Haslinger in 1892, and again the Emperor, to whom the work was dedicated, defrayed the expenses of publication out of his private purse.

Between March 1890 and March 1891 Bruckner turned his attention to his beloved Symphony No. 1 in C minor, his '*kecke Beserl*', and during the same year he also made some minor alterations in his 2nd Symphony and in the Mass in F minor. The position of the 1st Symphony is somewhat similar to that of No. 3. The work exists in two versions, both quite definitely from Bruckner's own pen and without additions or alterations on the part of any outsider: the 'Linz' version of 1865–66 (with minor alterations dating from 1868) and the 'Vienna' version of 1890–91. They stand side by side, are equally authentic, and it is impossible to argue for or against either version. Understandably the 'Vienna' version has gained much in detail owing to the experience which Bruckner had gathered in the intervening years, but on the other hand the 'Linz' version has more charm in its youthful freshness and its buoyancy.

With the completion of the 'Vienna' version of the 1st Symphony the long second period of revisions came to an end. It had taken much of Bruckner's time and energy, and it is not surprising that during those years only one new composition had come into being, the male chorus with tenor solo *Träumen und Wachen* of 1890. Nor were these years particularly eventful in Bruckner's private life. His days were filled with his duties at the Conservatorium, at the University, at the *Hofkapelle*, and with private pupils and his revision work, allowing only the occasional visit to Klosterneuburg. His holidays—and even they were 'working holidays'!—were spent in Upper Austria: St. Florian, Steyr, Kremsmünster, Vöcklabruck. In the public field things became somewhat quieter, and even the number of performances outside Austria diminished, possibly because Bruckner was so immersed in revising his existing works rather than writing new compositions. The only notable events during those years were the first 'all-Bruckner' concert in Vienna in January 1888, when Hans Richter conducted the 4th Symphony and the *Te Deum*, and a repeat performance of the 7th Symphony in February 1889, also in Vienna under Richter. It was in the same year that the Hellmesberger Quartet at long last performed Bruckner's String Quintet, which had meanwhile had so much success in so many other centres, and Karl Muck in Graz repeated the 7th Symphony.

Many of Bruckner's letters of this period voice a complaint which he had suffered from all his life—lack of time. Now, as he was nearing the end of his life, his situation in this respect was to become somewhat easier. He was the recipient of an annual grant from an Upper Austrian 'consortium' from 1889 onwards, the Emperor assisted him financially on several occasions, and in 1890 the Austrian goverment endowed him with an 'honorary stipend' of 400 guilders annually. In the following years his time-table also was to become less exacting, when he retired from the Conservatorium in 1891 and from the *Hofkapelle* in 1892. His lectures at the University, however, he kept up until 1894. On the other hand the effects of his illness became increasingly noticeable and compelled him to take six months' sick leave from the Conservatorium, from July 1890 until January 1891.

The year 1891 marks the beginning of the last period of Bruckner's life, the five years until his death in 1896. They are dominated almost entirely by the composition of his last great and unfinished symphony, No. 9. He had made sketches for the first movement as early as 1887, and in the beginning of 1889 he had sketched out the Scherzo, and also the Trio in F which he later rejected. It was not, however, until April 1891 that he settled down to uninterrupted work on the score which was to occupy him until the very last day of his life.

Happily, during this last creative period, Bruckner was to enjoy a series of triumphs in performances of his works. In December 1890 the 4th Symphony was given an enthusiastic reception at its first performance in Munich (under Franz Fischer, as Hermann Levi had fallen ill), and the same month brought the first performance of the 3rd Symphony in its third version under Hans Richter in Vienna. Now at last the Viennese audience made up for the disdain with which it had treated the 'Wagner Symphony' thirteen years earlier and accorded the aged composer an ovation. But the greatest triumph was yet to come, when on 31 May 1891 Siegfried Ochs performed the *Te Deum* in Berlin. Bruckner was present and received an acclaim which, according to all reports, was unprecedented in Berlin musical history. This visit to Berlin, incidentally, had one further consequence which was by no means unprecedented. In the Hotel Kaiserhof where he was staying he made the acquaintance of a chamber maid, Ida Buhz, and although he was by now well into his sixty-seventh year, he seriously considered marrying her. As was usual with Bruckner, anything illicit or secretive was out of the question, and while he was in Berlin he met her parents. He remained in correspondence with Ida and they met again on the occasion of Bruckner's second visit to Berlin in 1894, but the affair came to an end in 1895 through her refusal to change her Lutheran faith for Roman Catholicism.

After this Berlin trip Bruckner spent Easter at St. Florian, and the summer of 1891 and all the succeeding summers saw him again at St. Florian, Steyr, Linz, Kremsmünster and Vöcklabruck. In the autumn of 1891 Bruckner received the greatest honour of his life. On 7 November the University of Vienna conferred on him the Honorary Degree of Doctor of Philosophy. It was the first

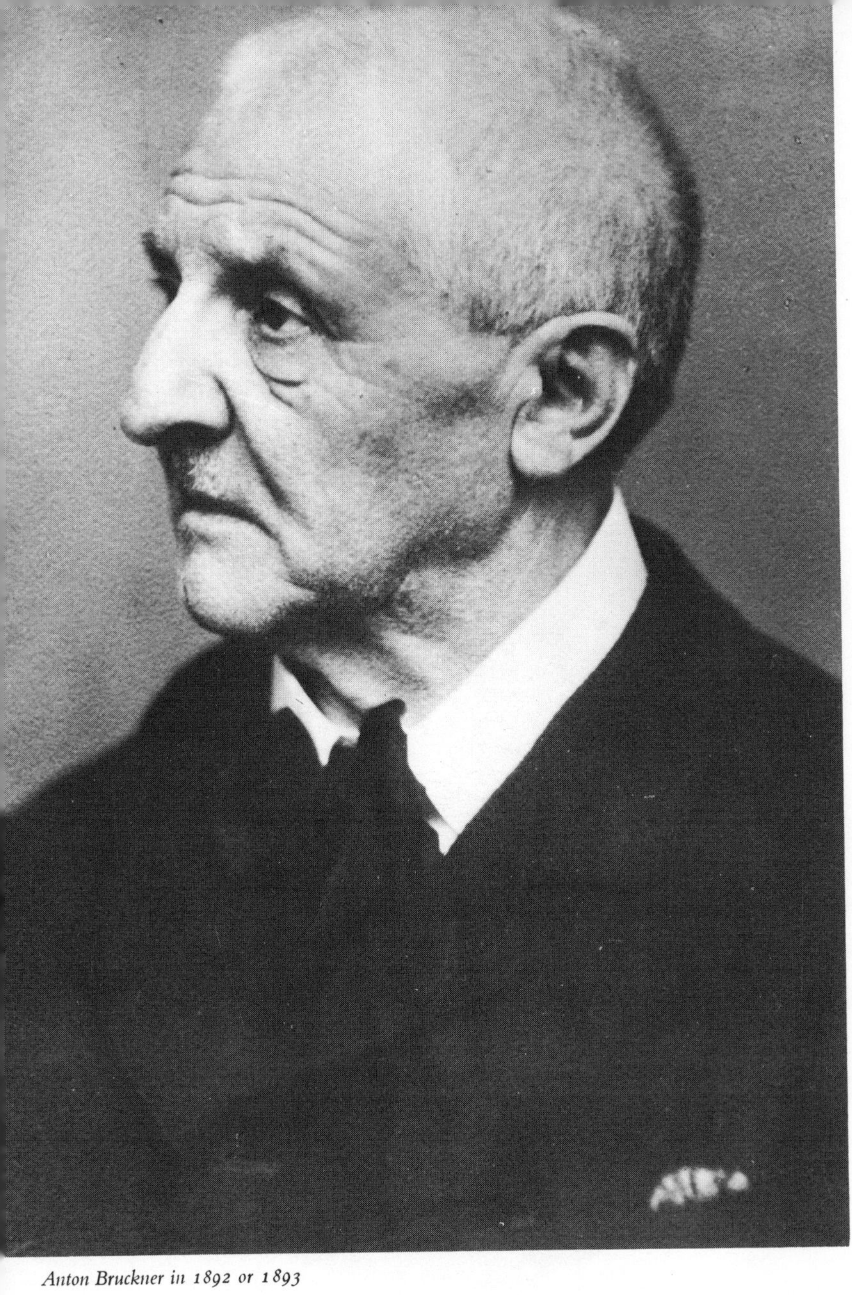

Anton Bruckner in 1892 or 1893

Anton Bruckner in 1894

time that this title had ever been bestowed in an honorary capacity on a musician. Bruckner was so overcome with emotion that when he tried to reply after the ceremony he completely lost the thread of his speech and finished in confusion: 'I cannot find the words to thank you as I would wish, but if there were an organ here, I could tell you.' Bruckner did in fact show his gratitude in the language which he spoke with such mastery, his music, by dedicating to the University the 'Vienna' version of his 1st Symphony, the first performance of which took place on 13 December 1891 under Hans Richter. One month after the official ceremony Bruckner was the guest of honour at a gala reception at which three thousand people were present, including the rector, Dr. Adolf Exner, who concluded his address with the now famous words: 'Where science must come to a halt, where its progress is barred by unsurmountable barriers, there begins the realm of art which knows how to express that which will ever remain a closed book to scientific knowledge. I, *Rektor magnificus* of the University of Vienna, bow humbly before the former assistant teacher of Windhaag.'

During 1892, while at work on the 9th Symphony, Bruckner composed three other works, the phrygian hymn *Vexilla Regis* for *a capella* chorus (first performed at St. Florian on Good Friday 1892), a male chorus with wind band accompaniment, *Das deutsche Lied*, and his last major religious composition, the 150th Psalm which, like the *Te Deum*, is scored for solo voices, chorus and orchestra. In 1893 he wrote his very last completed composition, a male chorus with orchestral accompaniment entitled *Helgoland*. This was the only one of his secular vocal compositions which Bruckner considered of sufficient artistic merit to be included amongst the scores which by his last will and testament he made over to the *Hofbibliothek*. During those last years Bruckner also toyed with the idea of composing an opera to a libretto by Gertrud Bollë-Hellmund with the title *Astra*. The subject had been selected from a noval *Die Toteninsel* by Richard Voss and was, as Bruckner had demanded, '*à la* Lohengrin, romantic, full of the mystery of religion, and completely free from all that is impure'. There, however, the matter rested. Bruckner never made as much as a preliminary sketch, and it remains an interesting matter for conjecture what an opera by Bruckner might have sounded like!

Meanwhile Bruckner's fame was spreading farther and farther afield. His music was played in most European countries as well as in America, and the 7th Symphony and the *Te Deum* particularly were greeted by storms of enthusiasm everywhere. Amongst the younger men who were coming increasingly to the fore as Bruckner conductors was Ferdinand Löwe, and particular mention must also be made of a conductor who contributed so greatly towards introducing Bruckner's music to America: Anton Seidl. Even Vienna began to realise that there was a genius living within its walls, and in the short period of five weeks, between 5 June and 9 July 1892, two symphonies were to be performed there: No. 4 and No. 3. Another great Vienna triumph for Bruckner came on 18 December 1892, when Hans Richter gave the first performance of the 8th Symphony. On this occasion not only the audience but even some

The Kustodenstöckl *in the Belvedere where Bruckner lived during the last two years of his life*

View over Vienna from the Upper Belvedere, with the spire of St. Stephen's Cathedral in the distance

sections of the otherwise hostile press greeted the work as that of a genius.[1]

On the publication side also matters advanced rapidly. The 2nd and 8th Symphonies and the D minor Mass were published in 1892, the 1st Symphony ('Vienna' version) in 1893, and the 5th Symphony in 1895. At the time of Bruckner's death No. 6 was the only completed symphony left unpublished. It finally came before the public in print in 1899.

Bruckner's health, however, was by now beginning seriously to deteriorate. In 1891 he heard the first *Festspielhaus* performance of *Tannhäuser*, and 1892 saw him in Bayreuth for the last time. Despite a serious spell of illness which kept him in bed in 1893 he was able to undertake the journey to Berlin in January 1894 in the company of Hugo Wolf in order to be present at a performance of the 7th Symphony as well as two performances of the *Te Deum*. At the first of these, on 8 January, Bruckner's name was for the first time bracketed with that of Hugo Wolf as composer, for at the same concert Wolf's choruses *Der Feuerreiter* and *Elfenlied* were also performed. However, he was not sufficiently well to attend the first performance of his 5th Symphony which Franz Schalk conducted in Graz on 8 April 1894. Bruckner was never to hear that symphony played by an orchestra, for his hope that Schalk would also play the work in Vienna was not to be fulfilled during his lifetime. On 12 January 1896 Bruckner was to hear a work of his own in concert performance for the last time, the *Te Deum*. It was the last concert he attended. By a curious coincidence (if it can be so called) the other two works that made up the programme were Wagner's *Liebesmahl der Apostel* and Richard Strauss' *Till Eulenspiegel*. Thus Bruckner's music was framed by that of the great master whom he had so revered and that of a young man who had just begun his ascent to fame.

Apart from the visits to Bayreuth and Berlin mentioned above, Bruckner's travels now took him no further afield than Upper Austria, and in those last years he spent much time in Steyr, St. Florian and Kremsmünster. He was also a frequent guest at Klosterneuburg near Vienna, where he spent Christmas 1893. After his retirement from the Conservatorium in 1891 and from the *Hofkapelle* in 1892 his time was much more his own, for his lectures at the University, which he continued until November 1894, had become somewhat sporadic owing to his frequent bouts of illness. But as a result of his retirement he also lost contact with many of his friends, and in those last years he often complained of loneliness. Some of his best friends were now in and around Steyr, and foremost amongst these was Franz Bayer, his former pupil and now *regens chori* at the Steyr *Stadtpfarrkirche* where, under his direction, the performance of Bruckner's D minor Mass was to become a regular Easter Day feature from 1893 onwards.

Bruckner spent his seventieth birthday in Steyr, far from the hustle and bustle of the Austrian capital, but whereas ten years earlier only the municipal band of Vöcklabruck had honoured the occasion publicly, now telegrams of

[1] A list of the many other performances which took place during the last years of Bruckner's life is given on pp. 83–85.

Last photograph of Anton Bruckner, taken at the Kustodenstöckl *in the company of his housekeeper 'Frau Kathi', his brother Ignaz and his physician Prof. Schrötter on 17 July 1896*

Steyr in about 1700

congratulation poured in from all over the world, the press devoted a lot of space to him to mark the occasion, and many organisations conferred honorary membership on him on that day. Vienna also honoured him with performances of his F minor Mass (4 November) and the 2nd Symphony (25 November). The state of his health was by now subject to severe fluctuations. On more than one occasion it seemed that his last hour had come, and by 1895 his mind had begun to wander at times. One consequence of his illness was that he became more and more hampered by shortage of breath, and it soon became virtually impossible for him to climb the stairs to his apartment on the fourth floor of Hessgasse 7. Once more the Emperor personally came to his assistance and put the *Kustodenstöckl*, a kind of gate-keeper's lodge, at *Schloss Belvedere* at his disposal, and this became Bruckner's last place of residence, from July 1895 until his death.

Although his speed of working was severely handicapped by his illness and by increasing age, Bruckner devoted all the energies of his last years to his Symphony No. 9 in D minor. The first sketches, as has been said, date back to 1887, and Göllerich reported that in the spring of 1889 Bruckner played him parts of the first movement. At the time, again according to Göllerich, he made

Bruckner's sarcophagus in the crypt of the Stiftskirche, *St. Florian*

the remark: 'It really annoys me that the theme of my new symphony came to me in D minor, because everybody will say now: "Of course, Bruckner's Ninth must be in the same key as Beethoven's!"' He began the full score in April 1891 and completed the first movement in October 1892, the Scherzo in February 1893, and the Adagio in November 1894. Throughout 1895 and 1896 he was engaged on the Finale, of which we have close on two hundred pages in the form of sketches, many of these already scored out. There is sufficient material available to give a clear idea of what he had in mind: this movement would have been the crowning glory of all his Finales with a strongly rhythmical first group of themes, a chorale, a fugue marking the beginning of the recapitulation and again the chorale, with the *Te Deum*

This stone flag in the porch of the Stiftskirche, *St. Florian, immediately below the Bruckner Organ, marks the spot where Bruckner's sarcophagus stands in the crypt beneath*

figurations, bringing the work to its apotheosis in the epilogue. But a 'completion' of the movement is unthinkable, and no one with the slightest love or respect for Bruckner would ever consider such a thing. Bruckner's fervent prayer was that he be granted enough time and energy to enable him to complete his 9th Symphony, but God in whose authority he believed so firmly and to whom the work was dedicated decreed otherwise. Until the very morning of 11 October 1896 Bruckner was at work on the Finale. Then God took the pen out of his hand, and it would be going against His will to try to add to the existing three movements which are so utterly complete in their incompletion.

In the 9th Symphony Bruckner's music takes on a truly visionary character. The first great theme with its crashing octave leap is perhaps the most monumental that Bruckner ever conceived, and the Scherzo is in an altogether different world from all his other Scherzi; nothing is left of the idea that every Bruckner Scherzo is a type of peasant dance. In the Adagio, which Bruckner himself termed the 'farewell to life' and in which passages reminiscent of his 7th and 8th Symphonies and of the Masses are heard, he touches on regions of spirituality, far removed from all earth-bound existence, that no ordinary mortal is ever permitted to see and experience during his lifetime.

On Sunday afternoon, 11 October 1896, in the *Kustodenstöckl* of the Belvedere, Anton Bruckner closed his eyes for ever. Three days later the funeral service in the *Karlskirche* was packed by a multitude paying their last respects to the great symphonist. But two of the greatest composers then living in Vienna, Johannes Brahms and Hugo Wolf, were absent. Wolf had been prevented from entering the church because he was not a member of one of the 'official' music associations, and Brahms, already severely ill himself, arrived late. When he was invited to enter the church, he merely shook his head and muttered some disjointed words which sounded like 'Never mind. Soon my coffin . . . ', and indeed it was only a matter of six months before Brahms followed Bruckner. At the funeral service the Adagio from the 7th Symphony, arranged for wind band by Löwe, was played— the great funeral music which Bruckner had written for his beloved 'master' Richard Wagner.

In deferrence to Bruckner's own wish his body was taken to St. Florian. From here he had gone out into the world, and in its monastic walls he came to his last rest. There, in a splendid sarcophagus, lie the earthly remains of Anton Bruckner, but from above the crypt, from the great 'Bruckner Organ', his living spirit still bursts forth in a thousand tongues:

IN TE, DOMINE, SPERAVI
NON CONFUNDAR IN AETERNUM!

His Character

In his article on Bruckner in *Die Musik in Geschichte und Gegenwart* Friedrich Blume writes: 'Whereas research into the work of Bruckner (especially through the efforts of R. Haas and A. Orel) has reached the true heart of the matter with sober textual elucidation and clarification, Bruckner's personality and character is still clouded over by the poisonous fumes of biased opinions. . . . Unconfirmed anecdotes, reputed utterances and conversations, rumours which have no known foundations are being dragged from one Bruckner biography into the next. For this reason every attempt to outline his true character must for the time being limit itself to a cautious approximation.' In this chapter we will examine the material at our disposal with caution in order to outline as far as possible the character of the man Bruckner which, to borrow the words of Schiller, has hitherto been '*von der Parteien Gunst und Hass verzerrt*', 'distorted by the favour and hatred of factions'.

In many publications, especially those which date from the earlier part of this century, Bruckner is variously represented as a more or less moronic village yokel, or as an ascetic monk, or as a combination of both. Obviously an injudicious choice of the sort of 'unconfirmed anecdotes' mentioned by Blume in his article is responsible for these misconceptions, and even a small measure of sober thought and serious consideration will lead one to quite another verdict.

The first of these misconceptions must be dealt with immediately, for it is the most flagrant and ridiculous one, if only for the simple reason that no 'country bumpkin' could possibly be at the same time the creative genius that Bruckner was. The contention that Bruckner was fundamentally a peasant is easily disproved if we look at his ancestry. We have to go back to his great-great-grandfather, to the end of the seventeenth century, to find a true peasant amongst his forebears, for his great-grandfather Josef was an innkeeper and broom-maker, and his grandfather (also named Josef) was a village school-

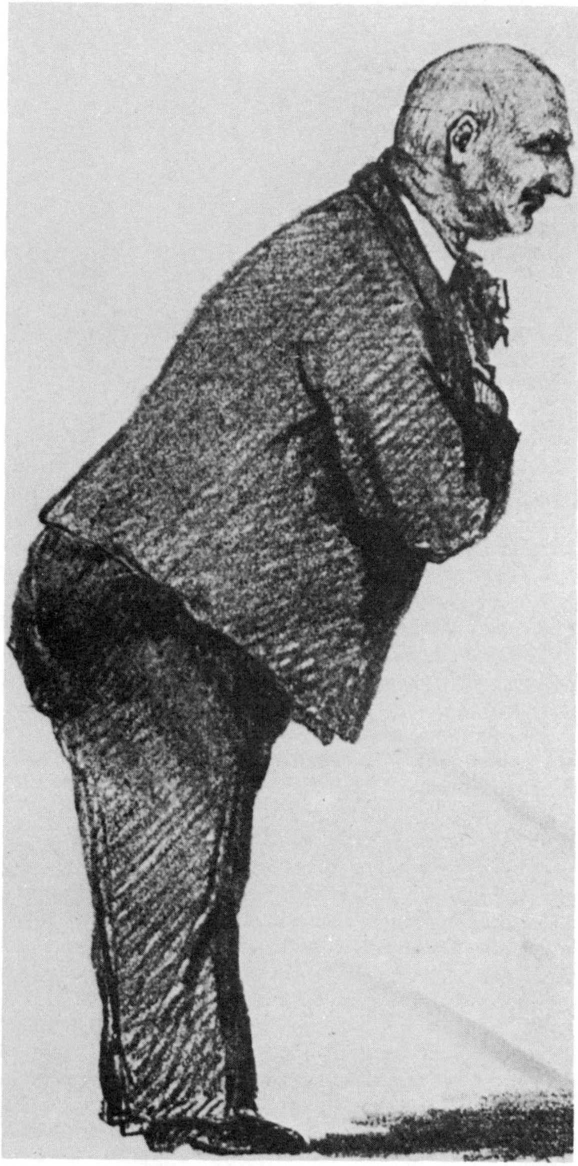

Caricature of Anton Bruckner, dated 21 March 1886

teacher. Bruckner himself was a third generation village schoolmaster, the stock which in Austria has so often been the cradle of musical genius. In every small Austrian community in those days the two persons who commanded the highest respect were the priest and the schoolteacher.

On the other hand it cannot be denied that, although Bruckner spent more than half his life in the cities of Linz and Vienna, he never became wholly acclimatised to city life. In his manner, his outward appearance and his whole attitude to life he always remained a rural type, and never conformed to the social niceties of cosmopolitan Vienna. His mode of dress in particular has given rise to derision: a white shirt with a very wide collar, for Bruckner liked to be comfortable, an equally generously cut black suit with rather short trouser legs so that he should not be hampered in playing the organ, and a wide-brimmed black slouch hat. The only 'artistic' touch to his dress was a loosely tied cravat. His physiognomy has also come in for a good deal of comment, and his profile has been described as 'a cross between that of an Austrian peasant and a Roman emperor'. In connection with the foregoing, the author had an interesting experience in the *Stiftskirche* of St. Florian in 1966. An elderly man, obviously a local inhabitant, with close cropped grey hair, a very pronounced profile, and dressed in the manner described above, entered the church and knelt in one of the pews. Had one had the temerity to intrude on his devotion with a camera, the resultant photograph could have been published over the caption 'Bruckner at prayer' without arousing the slightest comment. The incident shows that both in dress and in outward appearance Bruckner represented something which is essentially Upper Austrian and which persists to this day.

Similarly, his preference for the substantial dishes which are still the staple fare of every Austrian inn stemmed from the solid and unpretentious upbringing he had had as a child. By all accounts Bruckner had a gargantuan appetite, and it was by no means unknown for him to order two or even three helpings of the same dish at a sitting. From the evidence which we possess, however, it appears that, with all his teaching, organ playing and composing, Bruckner rarely found time for much eating during the day, and it was usually not until late evening that he finally settled down to his first proper meal. It is not surprising that by then he was ready for a hearty one. Moreover, although it is fairly well established that Bruckner was a great lover of Austrian wines and especially of Pilsen beer, there is no evidence in any of the multitudinous stories and anecdotes, whether true or invented, that he ever went beyond the borders of sobriety.

Kindheartedness and obvious enjoyment of all forms of conviviality were two further traits characteristic of Bruckner. His kindness must have had much the same simplicity as that of a teacher of young children. It is said that whenever he had a choir rehearsal at the *Hofkapelle*, he invariably brought bags of sweets in his capacious pockets for the choir boys. Ferdinand Edelhart, one of his organ pupils in Linz, tells of an occasion when he brought Bruckner the monthly fee for his lessons. A short while before Edelhart had deputised for

Restaurant 'Zu den drei Hackeln' near the Piaristenkirche, *where Bruckner often took his meals*

Bruckner at one of the two churches for which Bruckner was responsible, and now, to show his gratitude, Bruckner said, 'Do you know what? We're going to squander that today!' He ordered a sleigh and took Edelhart up to St. Florian, where they spent a happy evening at the inn. Outings such as this were a constant joy to Bruckner. They took him out of the monotony of his strenuous life and yet did not take up too much time, and whenever there was a special occasion he liked to celebrate it in this way. One particular instance which comes to mind was the excursion which Kitzler tells about. In 1863 Bruckner invited him and his wife to drive out to the inn *Jäger am Kürnberg* to celebrate the conclusion of the studies in musical form and orchestration on which he had been engaged with Kitzler. Strange as it may seem, Bruckner also appears to have been an enthusiastic and, by some accounts, quite proficient dancer, and there is frequent mention in the memoirs of his friends and students of his predilection for this kind of entertainment. Particularly during the carnival period he was a frequent guest at the various balls and similar functions, not only as a young man, but even when he was already well in his fifties. But perhaps the kind of social gathering which Bruckner most enjoyed was the evenings he spent with his pupils and his friends in the various inns of Linz and Vienna. These obviously meant a great deal to him; they were his way of relaxing after a hard day's work. Attendance at these 'sessions' was virtually mandatory for some of his pupils, and any absence was noted with decided displeasure. Conversation centred chiefly around music, but the atmosphere was gay, and Bruckner seems to have displayed a great sense of humour on these occasions. However, there is one point on which all those who later wrote about those evenings spent with Bruckner are in accord: he would not tolerate anything of a lewd or obscene nature, and whenever the joking or the general conversation tended in that direction, he would either put a stop to it or else take his leave in an ostentatious manner. Such convivial evenings were not spent solely in the circle of his *gaudeamus*, as he called the academic youth whose teacher he was, or of musical friends. He spent many evenings in academic circles, especially after he had been appointed lecturer at the University, and particularly amongst medical men.

Bruckner's interest in all matters pertaining to medicine, illness and death appears to have been very intense, and apparently in conversation on these subjects his questions were detailed and searching in the extreme. His interest in death, in fact, almost bordered on the morbid. He insisted on being present when Beethoven and Schubert were exhumed in the Währingen cemetery for reinterment at the central cemetery of Vienna, and when the *Ringtheater* was burned down in December 1881 with the loss of many lives he is reputed to have gone specially to the mortuary to see the charred remains of those who had died in the flames. These details are known only from the reports of others, but in one further instance we have his own incontestable evidence. Mexico had always been something of an obsession with him, and naturally he was most perturbed when Emperor Maximilian was executed in 1867. When it became known that Maximilian's body was to be brought back to Austria, he immediately wrote from Linz to his friend Rudolf Weinwurm in Vienna:

> 'At all costs I want to see the body of Maximilian. Please, Weinwurm, send someone reliable to the palace, or even better, make enquiries from the office of the *Oberhofmeister* whether it will be possible to see Maximilian's body, i.e. in an open coffin or under glass, or whether only the closed coffin will be visible. Then please let me know by telegram, so that I do not arrive too late. I ask you most urgently for this information'.[1]

Without wishing to attach undue importance to one letter, this does appear to give evidence of an extraordinary and insistent fascination. A passage from his

[1] Letter, 16 January 1868.

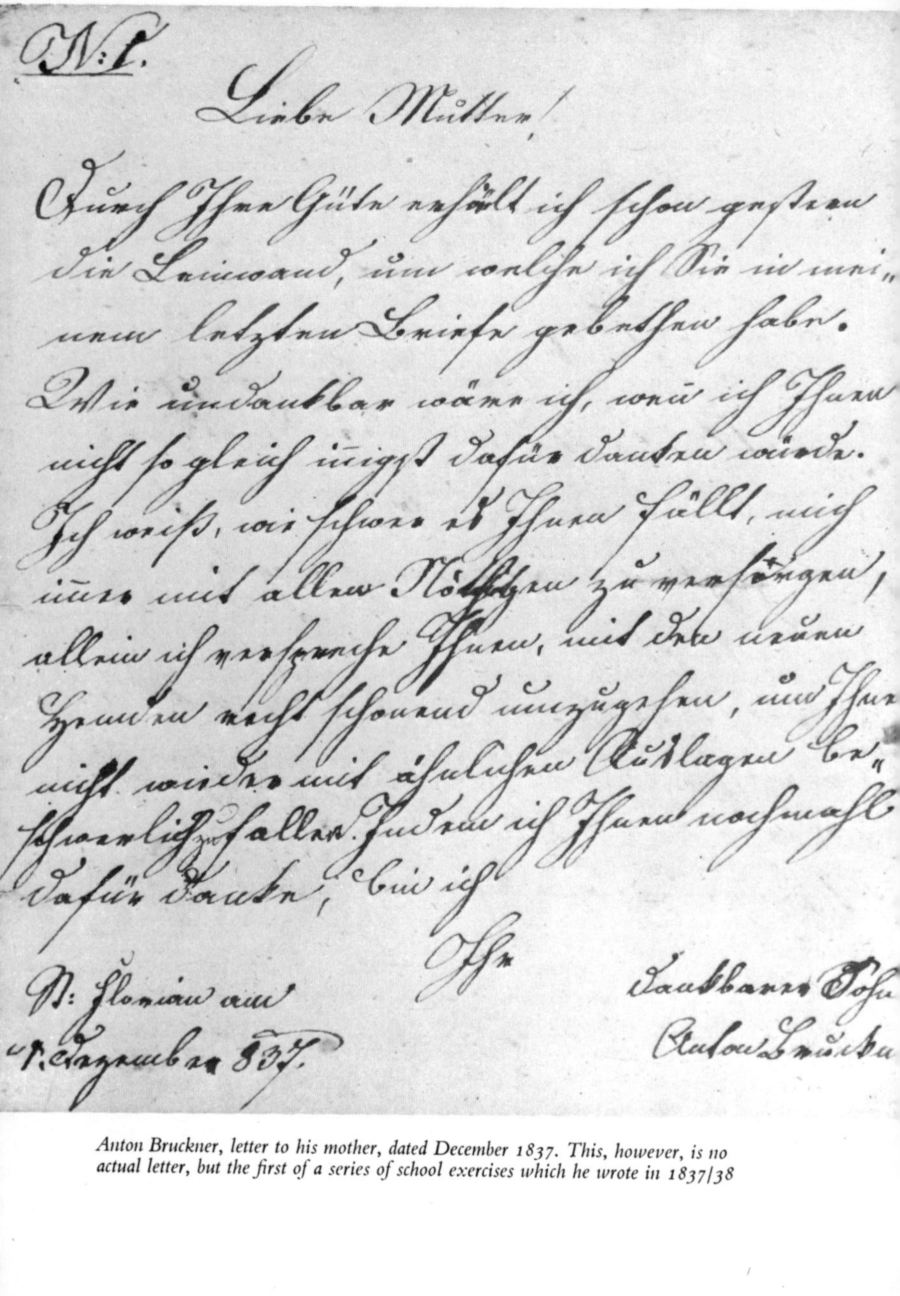

N: 1.

Liebe Mutter!

Durch Ihre Güte erhielt ich schon gestern die Leinwand, um welche ich Sie in meinem letzten Briefe gebethen habe. Wie undankbar wäre ich, wenn ich Ihnen nicht sogleich innigst dafür danken würde. Ich weiss, wie schwer es Ihnen fällt, mich immer mit allen Nöthigen zu versorgen, allein ich verspreche Ihnen, mit den neuen Hemden nicht schonend umzugehen, um Ihnen nicht wieder mit ähnlichen Auslagen beschwerlich zu fallen. Indem ich Ihnen nochmahl dafür danke, bin ich

Ihr

dankbarer Sohn
Anton Bruckner

St: Florian am
1. Dezember 837.

Anton Bruckner, letter to his mother, dated December 1837. This, however, is no actual letter, but the first of a series of school exercises which he wrote in 1837/38

will sheds further light on his detailed concern with death, this time his own:

> 'I wish my earthly remains to be placed in a metal coffin, this coffin to stand above ground in the crypt under the church of the Lateranensian *Chorherrnstift* St. Florian, immediately beneath the great organ. It is not to be interred, and permission has already been obtained during my lifetime from the Most Excellent Prelate of the said *Stift*. My body is to be embalmed, and Herr Professor Paltauf has kindly consented to do me this last kindness. All normal steps are to be taken (Class 1 funeral) that my body may be transferred to St. Florian in Upper Austria and put to rest in the place designated by me.'

Two particular characteristics which may possibly have been the chief factors in the creation of the prevailing misconceptions about Bruckner were his deference and his simplicity. His simplicity certainly bordered on the naïve, but it was more child-like than childish and it would be wrong to regard it as having been synonymous with lack of intelligence or culture. One instance has already been cited, the occasion when at the end of a rehearsal of his 4th Symphony he presented Hans Richter with a *Taler*, which certainly speaks for a certain unworldliness. In 1892, when the 8th Symphony had its first performance, Hans Richter was again the recipient of a present of a somewhat unusual nature. Bruckner is reputed to have awaited Richter at the artists' entrance with forty-eight piping hot *Krapfen*, a type of large doughnut, which he intended them to eat together to celebrate the performance. Whether the story is true or not it fits other facts which are known with greater certainty, but whether to smile at its child-like warmheartedness, or to be disdainful, is very much a matter of individual opinion.

His deference is a different matter; for this there is a lot of evidence, not only from the reports of his contemporaries but also from his own letters. His mode of address was burdened with terms of respect and devotion, and this has given rise to the belief that he was servile. Here again it must not be overlooked that he came of a village schoolmaster's family, that his character was formed before the revolution of 1848, and that at the time of that revolution he was at St. Florian and felt neither its immediate nor its after-effects. Nor was he, unlike Beethoven or Brahms for instance, imperturbably confident about his ability as a composer, at least not in the earlier stages of his life. Bruckner began his rise to fame at a time of life when most other composers had already reached their peak, and by that time the customs and usages so firmly implanted in a child of the pre-1848 world had become second nature and could no longer be shaken off. In that pre-1848 world social behaviour, correct forms of address, precedence and the like were laid down to a nicety and would certainly have been hammered into the head of a schoolmaster's child, and although there is no doubt that Bruckner was a fundamentally modest person, many of the flowery and even, to our way of thinking, subservient forms of address that he used were merely the conventional formulae which came to him auto-

Simon Sechter (1788–1867), Bruckner's teacher

Simon Sechter's 'Grundsätze der musikalischen Komposition' (*The Principles of Musical Composition*), *Vol. I, p. 74, with Bruckner's own marginal notes*

oder auch, uneigentlicherweise, durch den falschen Dreiklang der 2ten Stufe vorbereitet; seine Auflösung erhält er durch den Dur-Dreiklang oder den gleichartigen Septaccord der 3ten Stufe u. s. w. Z. B. in A moll:

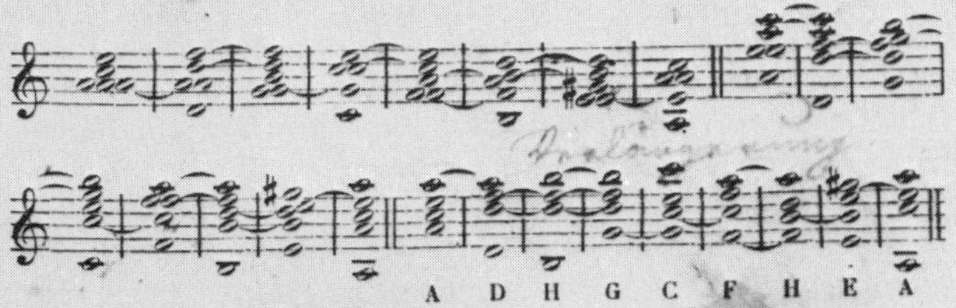

NB. Bei dem letzten Beispiele vertritt der Dreiklang auf *H* im dritten Tact nur den darauf folgenden Septaccord auf *G*.

9. Der Septaccord der 7ten erhöhten Stufe erhält seine Vorbereitung ganz wie der vorige. Seine Auflösung als selbstständiger Accord erhält er durch die zweite Verwechslung des übermässigen Dreiklangs und des gleichartigen Septaccordes der 3ten Stufe; was sodann noch zu folgen hat, ist bekannt. Z. B. in A moll:

10. Der Septaccord der 4ten Stufe mit kleiner Terz wird durch den Dreiklang oder Septaccord der 1ten Stufe, oder durch den Dreiklang der 6ten natürlichen Stufe vorbereitet; er kann sich aber nur in den Septaccord der natürlichen oder erhöhten 7ten Stufe oder deren zweite Verwechslung auflösen u. s. w. Z. B. in A moll:

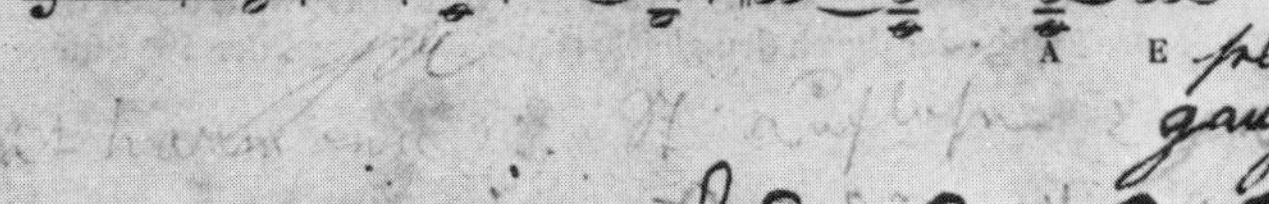

matically. They were not intended to convey servility, and there was nothing extraordinary in Bruckner's use of them. Bruckner, moreover, could sometimes be devastatingly direct. The abbot Leander of Kremsmünster tells of the day Bruckner gave an organ recital in the monastery church. On leaving the church Bruckner asked him, 'Well, Father Leander, how did you like it?' to which the priest replied: 'Professor, you mustn't ask me, for in musical matters I am a complete ass.' Bruckner's laconic comment was: 'Console yourself, you aren't the only one!'[1] Perhaps the nearest approach to an assessment of this side of Bruckner's character would be to say that he was of an almost Parsifal-like unworldliness, something like Wagner's 'pure fool'.

Bruckner's belief in the absolute validity of authority likewise stems from the pre-1848 era, when social values and gradations were unshakable. Taken in combination with the slightly pedantic turn of mind Bruckner had acquired both by inheritance and by his own training as a teacher, the reason for much of his behaviour becomes clear, above all for his obsession to possess certificates and diplomas to prove that he had completed this or that course of studies. In his life everything had to be well ordered and regulated; there was nothing of the bohemian in him. This attitude finds expression in his scores. Leaving aside the vexing question of the 'versions', his scores are models of clarity and there can never be the slightest doubt as to his intentions in them. Deletions are clearly marked with the words *gilt nicht* ('not valid'), the numbering of the bars makes his periodic structure perfectly obvious, and there is hardly another composer who peppered his scores to such an extent with accidentals in order to exclude every conceivable ambiguity. There is none of that slovenliness which is popularly regarded as the mark of genius. His scores stand with those of Bach and Wagner as models of neatness and precision. In other fields, of course, his childlike faith in the absolute power of authority was touching and even humorous. There is an unconfirmed story of an audience with the Emperor. According to this anecdote, the Emperor asked Bruckner at the end of the audience whether there was anything else he could do for him, and Bruckner supposedly asked the Emperor to stop Hanslick being so damaging in his press reports. Again it is immaterial whether the story is true or not, for even as a parable it illustrates the blind faith which Bruckner had in the authority of the 'Highest in the Land'.

It was similarly the era and environment of his childhood and the complete absence of any bohemian element in his psychological make-up that determined his attitude to financial matters and security. The fact that as a boy of twelve he had had to deputise for his sick father as the bread-winner of the family also contributed to this attitude. Throughout his life he worried about what would happen to him in old age, and whenever he contemplated a change of position one of his first queries was about pension rights. While he was still in Linz he took out an insurance policy to provide for his old age. The fact is, however, that though his financial position was a constant source of worry to

[1] From Altman Kellner, *Musikgeschichte des Stiftes Kremsmünster*, Bärenreiter Verlag, Kassel & Basel, 1956, p. 763–4.

Cosima and Richard Wagner with Franz Liszt and Hans von Bülow (seated on extreme right). Painting by W. Beckmann

him, he was never actually all that badly off. He was never rich, and his compositions earned him precious little, but from the moment he left the *Präparandie* in Linz in 1841 up until his death he was never without a regular income of some description, however small it may have been, and the bare necessities of livelihood were always assured. How different from his great Austrian brother-composer, Franz Schubert, who throughout his life never knew a moment's financial security! It is in fact in such a comparison that the character and basic attitudes of Bruckner become clearest. To Bruckner the very thought of being in debt was anathema, whereas Schubert, who in his pronouncedly bohemian outlook was the complete antithesis of Bruckner, went gaily through life in a happy-go-lucky way, never losing a night's sleep simply because he had been compelled once more to borrow money from some source or other. In a way the contrast between the two composers is strange, for both came from the same environment, a schoolmaster's family, though Schubert's home did not lie in such rural surroundings. It was, of course, mainly a difference in temperament; Schubert was eternally optimistic whereas Bruckner tended to melancholy and pessimism. It should not, however, be overlooked that Schubert did not have the same depressing experiences as Bruckner did after the death of his father and during his Windhaag period, and that Schubert died at thirty-one—the age at which Bruckner was just moving from St. Florian to Linz to embark upon his musical career.

Uncertainty, lack of self-assurance, is another characteristic attributed to Bruckner, and of his personal life this was certainly true. It has been shown how the prospect of change threw him into a panic of indecision, as for example at those two major turning points of his life, when he left St. Florian for Linz in 1855, and later when he was called from Linz to Vienna in 1868. Such changes represented appalling upheavals in his well-ordered life. In addition to the actual change involved the matter was further fraught with financial considerations. When it comes to his music, however, the position is somewhat different. It is true that in early life he was unsure of himself even in composition, for to him the rules and regulations of Sechter and his other teachers were sacrosanct, and he would no more have considered breaking these rules than he would have considered open revolution. His utter belief in authority, in fact, acted as a brake on his own inspiration: we know for instance that, after he had finished his studies with Kitzler and was already at work on his 1st Symphony in C minor, he showed a passage to the violinist Ignaz Dorn and asked: 'My dear Dorn, do have a look at this. Is one permitted to write that?' But once he was armed with all the requisite 'certificates' of his proficiency as a composer, he soon overcame this lack of self-assurance and composed with the utter conviction that what he wrote down was right and was the way he wanted it. Nor is the preceding statement affected by the two periods he spent revising his works. In the first of these it was basically the inner urge towards perfection which spurred him on,[1] whereas in the second

[1] But see footnote on p. 89.

Bruckner's close friend Rudolf Weinwurm (died 1911)

Letter from Bruckner to the priest of the Stadtpfarrkirche, Steyr

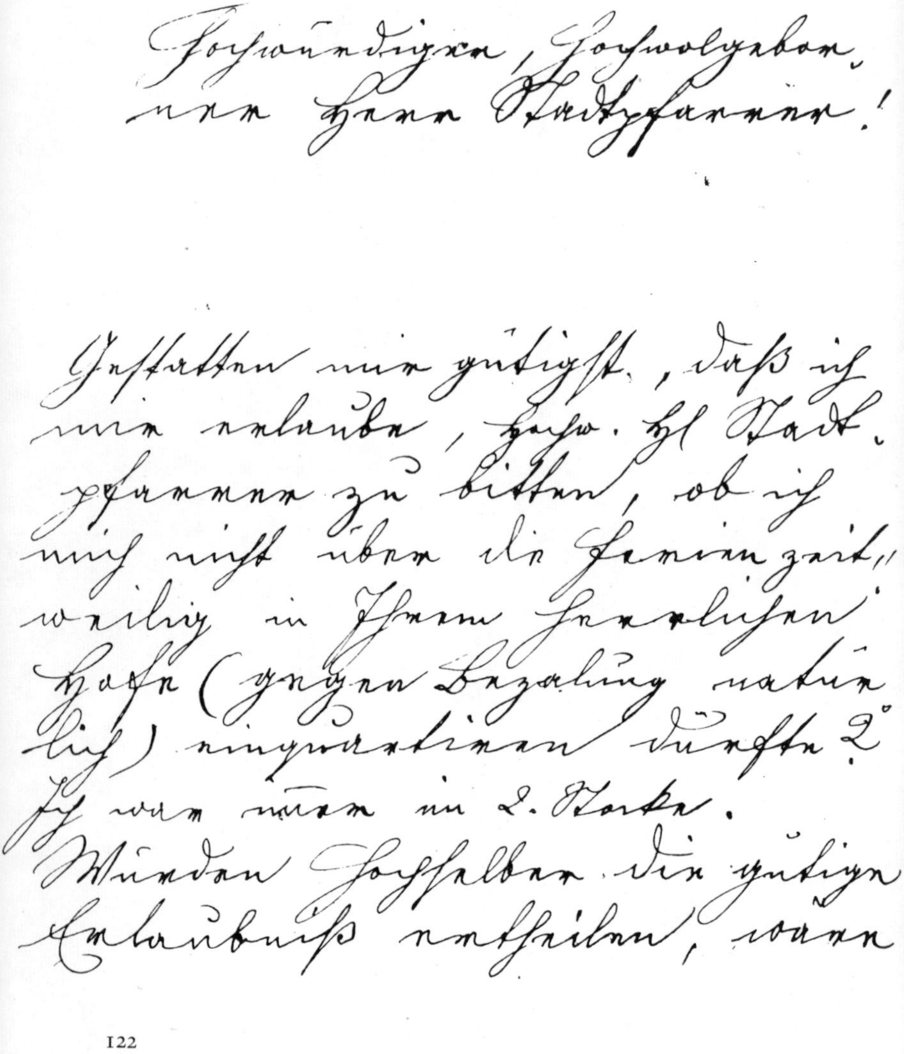
Hochwürdigster, Hochwohlgeboren,
euer Herr Stadtpfarrer!

Gestatten mir gütigst, daß ich mir erlaube, Hochw. Hl Stadtpfarrer zu bitten, ob ich mich nicht über die Ferienzeit, weilig in Ihrem herrlichen Hofe (gegen Bezahlung natürlich) einquartieren dürfte? Ich war neu im 2. Kurse.
Würden Hochselber die gütige Erlaubniß ertheilen, wäre

ich sehr glücklich darüber.
Ich suche nun Luft- und
Ruhe, da ich recht fleißig
an meiner 8. Sinfonie
zu componiren habe. Ein
Pianino würde ich wohl be-
kommen können, u. im Hause
Niemanden stören, da ich
nur das Niederzuschreibende
spielen, außer dem, äußerst
wenig. Nächste Woche geden-
ke ich von Wien abzureisen.
Ich wohne: I. Bezirk, Heßgasse
No 7. Bitte um gnädige
Antwort. Mit tiefstem Respekt
Wien, 1. Juli 1885. A. Bruckner m/p

he was under great pressure, and this at a time when his self-confidence was somewhat shaken by Levi's rejection of the 8th Symphony. Bruckner was nevertheless exceedingly stubborn, and again and again we hear from Herbeck, from Schalk and from Löwe what extraordinary efforts they had to make to get Bruckner to agree to alterations or cuts. That Bruckner was absolutely sure of himself even when he did give in to the well-meaning advice and insistence of his friends is shown quite clearly by what he said on many occasions: that his symphonies as *he* had written them were meant for 'times to come'—a statement which has fortunately been handed down to us not only in the reports of others, but in his own letters as well, so that here the evidence is conclusive. When he allowed those around him to influence him in the matter of cuts and alterations, it was not a sign of weakness (Bruckner himself had referred to his 'Upper Austrian stubbornness'!), but merely a concession to the spirit and the demands of his time. The accusation might therefore be levelled at him that he committed the artistic crime of compromise, but he wanted his symphonies to be performed, his music to be heard, and to this end the sacrifices must have appeared worthwhile to him. After all, in death he was to have the last word when he confided his precious manuscripts in the form in which he considered them valid to the *Hofbibliothek* in anticipation of those 'times to come'.

From time to time aspersions have also been cast on his general level of learning and his literary style. It is true that, as far as can be gathered, he had no time for 'small talk' and took scant interest in the world around him, and his library by all accounts contained only religious matter and works on music, as well as two other books, one dealing with the Mexican war, the other with a North Pole expedition (another subject which seems to have had considerable fascination for Bruckner). Nor was he particularly interested in the great literature of his century. But his erudition is in no way affected by this or put in any doubt, for after all he had taken both the primary and the advanced course of the *Präparandie*, the teachers' training college, and later in life he studied various subjects unrelated to music. In 1847 he immersed himself in studies of Latin and physics, and during the time in 1853 when he worked in a voluntary capacity as a clerk at the local court he must have acquired a certain amount of legal knowledge. Also his great interest in scientific matters is shown by a complaint made when he was assistant teacher in Windhaag. He had had the temerity to tell his children about the motions of the sun and moon in relation to the earth, and in those pre-1848 days teachers were not allowed to introduce such 'controversial' matter into their lessons. Quite apart from the foregoing, however, it seems inconceivable that the people of academic rank with whom, and this is known for certain, he associated socially in Vienna would have suffered his continued presence if he had not been able to conduct a reasonably intelligent conversation. The style of his letters, apart from the deferential terminology which has already been discussed, is simple and direct, in contrast to that of such 'literary musicians' as Wagner and Schumann for instance. In fact one cannot quite rid oneself of a feeling that

Hugo Wolf

Johann von Herbeck, one of Bruckner's first supporters

their letters were written with half an eye to posthumous publication. But a simple style is not synonymous with a poor style. Bruckner's letters are free from mistakes in grammar and spelling, and his handwriting is certainly not that of an uneducated person. However, all doubt on this subject can be dispelled in a far simpler manner: on 25 November 1875 Bruckner delivered an oration at the University of Vienna when he took up his lectureship in harmony and counterpoint, and no one who has read the text of this oration (which unfortunately is too lengthy to be quoted within the scope of this book) will have any doubts as to Bruckner's education and culture.

Throughout his life Bruckner considered himself unjustly persecuted; his letters are full of complaints about the lack of performances of his works and the hostility of the critics. This subject has been given great prominence in most of the biographies, where he is usually depicted as being utterly maltreated, and his life a complete misery. It is true that he was deeply hurt by the way in which he was ignored by many sections of the musical world, by the hostile treatment which was meted out to him by Hanslick and his circle in Vienna, and by the almost total absence of any material recognition of his work. His resentment must have been considerably aggravated by the way in which Brahms, in the same city, was continually triumphant, with publishers paying him colossal sums for each and every work. And when we consider the innate melancholy and depressive tendencies of Bruckner's character, it cannot be denied that he must have suffered a great deal of misery and frustration as a result of this lack of recognition. But looked at objectively almost a century later, his unending complaints do seem to be somewhat exaggerated. One point which is hardly ever taken into consideration, and which would appear to have a vital bearing on the question, is the fact that Bruckner only began his real career as a composer at the age of forty, with his D minor Mass, an age at which most other composers were already established, and indeed many of them had completed or were nearing the end of their life span. It is only natural that it takes every composer a certain number of years, from the moment that he first presents himself to his public, to make his name, and it is not surprising that in Bruckner's case, having started so late, recognition and international acclaim did not come until he had reached the age of sixty. This sober thought, if it ever occurred to him, must have been small consolation, but on the other hand, despite the love and admiration one may feel for Bruckner, it is no good ignoring obvious facts. Also, the actual number of performances of his major works during his lifetime was not in fact all that small. The following list[1] of all his major compositions indicates in each case how many years[2] elapsed between their completion and Bruckner's death, and the number of performances known to have taken place during those years:

[1] Taken from Gerh. F. Wehle: *Anton Bruckner im Spiegel seiner Zeitgenossen*, G. E. Schroeder-Verlag, Garmisch-Partenkirchen, 1964. See also p. 83.

[2] The first figure refers to the completion of the first version, the figure in brackets to the completion of the final revision.

Anton Bruckner in about 1885

Anton Bruckner wearing the Order of Franz Josef which the Austrian Emperor bestowed on him in 1886

D minor Mass	32 years	14 performances
E minor Mass	30 ,,	3 ,,
F minor Mass	29 ,,	13 ,,
Te Deum	12 ,,	30 ,,
String Quintet	17 ,,	23 ,,
Symphony No. 1	30 ,,	5 ,,
No. 2	24 ,,	6 ,,
No. 3	23 (19) ,,	24 ,,
No. 4	22 (16) ,,	19 ,,
No. 5	19 ,,	3 ,,
No. 6	15 ,,	1 ,,
No. 7	13 ,,	32 ,,
No. 8	9 (6) ,,	3 ,,

As will be seen from the foregoing, Bruckner had a fair number of performances to his credit by October 1896, although of course many of these date from the last twelve years of his life, commencing with the memorable Leipzig performance under Nikisch of the 7th Symphony. The same reasoning applies to a certain extent to the treatment which he received from the press. It must be admitted that Hanslick and his followers were consistently and openly hostile to Bruckner right up to the end and must have inflicted incalculable hurt on him by their vicious attacks, especially since they were the most powerful clique in Vienna's musical life in those days. On the other hand, however, there was a band of writers who were frankly pro-Bruckner, foremost amongst them Ludwig Speidel who was Bruckner's constant supporter from 1858 onwards, and later Hugo Wolf. There is an amusing letter which Bruckner wrote to Dr. van Meurs in Holland in February 1885, in which he first complains about the bad treatment given him by the press and then lists those papers which view his music in a favourable light—and quite an imposing list it is: '. . . but in Vienna the entire musical clique considers me an outcast (with the exception of the *Deutsche Zeitung*, the *Fremdenblatt*, the *Tagesblatt*, the *Morgenpost* and the musical periodicals).' This is not to minimise Bruckner's suffering, for suffer he undoubtedly did, but it does show that the cause did not lie solely in the situation as such, but derived to some extent from Bruckner's temperament.

Another topic which must be discussed in connection with Bruckner's character is his relations with women. There is no other aspect of Bruckner's personality about which more has been written. All kinds of theses have been advanced, and Freudian terminology has been liberally applied. Yet the matter does not appear to be so very complex. It seems quite certain that out of his deep religious belief Bruckner lived a life of self-imposed celibacy, and that any form of physical contact with a woman was repellent to him unless sanctioned by holy matrimony. Naturally it is impossible to prove this point,

Karl Muck (1859–1940) who gave frequent performances of Bruckner's symphonies

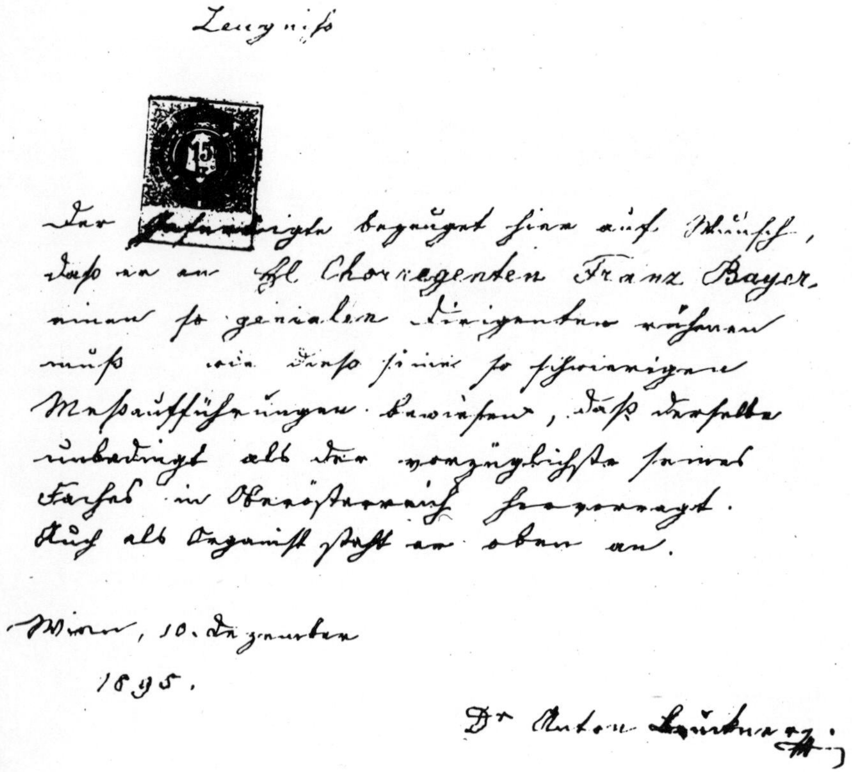

Zeugniß

Der Gefertigte bezeugt hiemit auf Wunsch,
daß er am Hl. Chorregenten Franz Bayer
einen so genialen Dirigenten rühmen
muß wie dass seine so schwierigen
Meßaufführungen beweisen, daß derselbe
unbedingt als der vorzüglichste seines
Faches in Oberösterreich hervorragt.
Auch als Organist steht er oben an.

Wien, 10. Dezember
1895.

Dr Anton Bruckner m.p.

Reference which Bruckner wrote for Franz Bayer

but the assumption is strengthened by the fact that there is not one single story, one single rumour to disprove it, and it is well known that in this context especially, rumours sprout in superabundance if there is even the scantiest basis for them. Throughout his adult life Bruckner was repeatedly attracted to members of the fair sex, especially girls in their late teens, and courting them, proposing and being rejected were such a constant occurrence in his life that this became a standing joke amongst his friends. Yet to all appearances these rejections never had any very deep or lasting effect on him, and they certainly never affected his musical work. He saw a pretty girl, his love flared up, and when the inevitable rebuff came the flame was extinguished almost as quickly as it had risen. It is true that he always hankered after the comforts of married life. In November 1885, when he was sixty-one, he wrote to Moritz von Mayfeld: '. . . As for my getting married, I have no bride to date. If only I could find a really suitable, dear girl!' Nor will it ever be possible to assess what inner battles, what efforts of self-discipline this celibacy cost him. It would seem, however, that his approaches to women and girls were dictated far more by a pursuit of the *Ewig-weibliche*, the 'eternal feminine', the creative principle in Goethe's meaning, than by the mere physical consideration, to which must of course be added the more practical wish for a home, a well-ordered household. A clue to the whole complex may be found in a remark quoted by Kitzler, who visited Bruckner in 1874 and, aghast at the untidiness of Bruckner's apartment, suggested that he should get married. Bruckner replied: 'My dear friend, I have no time. I must write my 4th Symphony!' Perhaps that is the answer: Bruckner's entire life, every fibre of his being, was absorbed by his music. There was just no time for anything else.

One important aspect has not yet been touched upon, and because of its very importance it has been left until last: Bruckner's religion. This again is a subject which has given rise to endless polemic and a great deal of misconception, particularly the idea that Bruckner was a 'monkish' type. It is interesting to note that, when the prior of St. Florian gave the fifteen-year-old boy the option of becoming a teacher or entering Holy Orders, young Anton decided without a moment's hesitation in favour of teaching, and there is no evidence whatsoever that he regretted this decision at any time in his later life. He loved the monastic atmosphere of St. Florian, Kremsmünster and Klosterneuburg; of that there can be no doubt. He belonged, however, to the world and its pleasures. His desire to marry, for instance, remained with him throughout his life.

His religion was a personal and private matter. Born and brought up as he was in the Catholic faith, that faith became an integral part of him, and a more fervent and unquestioning believer it is hard to imagine. To him God was not something mystical and nebulous but a reality; someone to whom he could turn for comfort in every distress and whose praises he sang in every note of his music. He followed and obeyed the dictates of his faith neither for the sake of conventionality nor through compulsion, but out of an inner urge springing from a deep conviction of their essential rightness. Just as he had absolute

Vienna, Karlskirche

In diesem Hause starb
ANTON BRUCKNER
am 11. Oktober 1896.

Plaque on the Kustodenstöckl *to mark Bruckner's death there on 11 October 1896*

In this way Bruckner kept an account of his daily prayers,. The abbreviation A = *Ave Maria*, C = *Credo*, S = *Salve Regina*, V = Lord's Prayer (*Vaterunser*), and the symbol ≠ signifies the rosary. By the underlinings Bruckner kept a record of the number of times he said each prayer.

confidence in worldly authority, so his faith was an immutable factor in his life. One cannot but admire a man who took his religion so seriously as to keep a daily account in his diary of the number of his prayers. Of Bruckner's innermost religious feelings comparatively little is known, as he seems to have spoken rarely about religious matters, and his friends and pupils all assert that they themselves studiously avoided the subject as being that on which it was easiest to arouse Bruckner's anger and displeasure. From the many and varied reports from different sources, however, it is possible to gain an idea, for these are certain points on which all his chroniclers agree. Whenever Bruckner improvised on the organ, he spent some time in prayer beforehand, and by all accounts this was no mere word-saying but a complete immersion in a meditative process which took him beyond the confines of the physical world. Bruckner's pupils speak of times when in the middle of a lesson they suddenly became aware that his mind and spirit were no longer with them: the church bells had rung, and Bruckner was praying.

Another anecdote may also serve to show that to Bruckner religion was not something which belonged to the church only and was confined to Sundays, but was a living factor permeating his entire life. In one of his lectures Bruckner noticed a Jewish student sitting in the hall. He went up to him, placed a hand on his head and said: 'Do you really believe that the Messiah has not yet come?'

In short, it seems that Bruckner lived as a perfectly normal human being, enjoying all the pleasures of life provided that they were not sinful, but that all his actions were dictated by the basic precepts of his faith, that his devotions were as real and essential a part of his life as his food and sleep, and that his prayers were never mere lip service but concentrated meditation in which he may have attained visionary realms which found their expression in his music.

His Music

It was said at the outset that 'the story of Bruckner's life is virtually synonymous with the story of the growth of his music'. The man and his music are indeed inseparable; it is impossible to draw a strict dividing line between his life and his work, and some overlapping is unavoidable. Much information regarding his musical output is already contained in the foregoing. Nor is it the purpose of this book to give a searching and detailed analytical account of his works: that would be a gigantic task going far beyond the scope of this book. What is intended here is to give a general survey and assessment of Bruckner's music, to point out and elucidate those characteristics which are most peculiar to it, and to deal in the main with those works which are most frequently performed, with particular emphasis on that form which Bruckner made his own: the symphony.

From this point of view the vast majority of compositions written before 1864 can be ignored. For the most part they are workmanlike pieces which show that their composer knew the basic rules and craft of composition, but their intrinsic value is not in any way outstanding; they could equally well have been written by any other schoolmaster and organist of that period provided he had a reasonable technical grounding and average talent. It is true that in certain works there is already evidence of a type of harmonic structure, a tendency towards dissonance and somewhat unusual modulations, which was later to become so typical of Bruckner (in this context the *Sanctus* and *Agnus* of the Kronstorf Mass of 1844 come to mind particularly), but it would be an exaggeration to see in these relatively isolated instances the hallmark of budding genius. These early works are of interest to the Bruckner scholar but would have no place in the present-day concert hall.

Similarly there is no need to dwell on his songs and small-scale works for one or two instruments, and in any case these represent only a very small part of his output: half a dozen songs, the *Abendklänge* for violin and piano (1866), and a number of pieces for piano solo or piano duet. Most of the piano pieces are little dances, and like the songs they all have a certain charm, but they bear little relationship to the type of music which automatically comes to mind when the name of Bruckner is mentioned. The same holds good for his organ music, of which there is astonishingly little: apart from the small preludes which he wrote at the age of about twelve, and of some of which the authenticity is doubtful, we only possess five organ compositions from Bruckner's hand. With the exception of one C major Prelude for Harmonium (1884) they are all early works and are, generally speaking, devoid of interest. Even the latest of these organ pieces proper, the Fugue in D minor of 1861, gives no evidence of any true inspiration. It is academically correct but completely arid and could be the homework of any conservatorium student who had mastered the rules of counterpoint and fugue and applied them painstakingly. This is strange in view of the greatness which Bruckner indubitably achieved on the instrument, and the only explanation is that being such an uncontested master of improvisation he could not be bothered to write down on paper the music which flowed from him so readily when he sat on the organ bench. Of course this is only an assumption, but it is in conformity with his remark[1] that in London he would leave the playing of Bach to those organists whose lack of imagination did not allow them to improvise freely.

In the field of secular choral music Bruckner composed a large number of works: 33 male choruses, two of which have orchestral accompaniment, and 3 mixed choruses. This predominance of compositions for male chorus is explained by the fact that the vast majority of choral associations in Austria and Germany were exclusively male, a state of affairs which persists to the present day. This presumably is also the reason why these works are hardly ever heard outside the German-speaking countries, quite apart from the language barrier. Most of them were occasional compositions, as is indicated by the texts in many cases, and there is no evidence that Bruckner attached any special importance to them, with the exception of the two choruses with orchestral accompaniment: the *Germanenzug* of 1863 and *Helgoland* of 1893. The former is the work which in later years Bruckner described as 'his first real composition'; the latter, composed only three years before his death, he included in the precious package of scores which he bequeathed to the *Hofbibliothek*. These are the only two of his choral compositions which Bruckner considered worth mentioning in his letters to friends whenever a performance had taken place.

His sacred choral music is a different matter, for this represents the expression of Bruckner's faith and deepest beliefs. Here is nothing of a 'casual' or 'occasional' nature; each of these works came from his heart, and their relative merit depends only upon the stage which his own musical development had reached at the time. Small-scale compositions such as motets, cantatas and the like are in marked preponderance. From the very beginning Bruckner composed

[1] See above, p. 52.

First page of the autograph of the Requiem

short works for church services, and many of them are still in everyday use in the churches of Austria. Here we find a Bruckner who is vastly different from the Bruckner of the great Symphonies and Masses. For example, it is in some of these short works that his heritage of the great period of vocal polyphony, the period of Palestrina, Lassus and Lotti, becomes most apparent. Again most of the earlier compositions, though many of them are exceedingly well written, show no sign of Bruckner's individuality, but the seven-part *Ave Maria* of 1861 can perhaps be described as the first work of the mature Bruckner. It is outstanding for its purity of line and its mastery of contrapuntal interweaving, and despite the fact that its Palestrinian ancestry is undeniable it is also filled with that glowing devotion which characterises so much of Bruckner's religious music. It was followed by the beautiful phyrgian *Pange lingua* and the *Asperges me* of 1868, and the Vienna years brought forth those great motets *Locus iste* (1869), *Tota pulchra* (1878), the lydian *Os justi* and the second *Christus factus est* (1879), the third *Christus factus est* and *Salvum fac* (1884), *Virga Jesse* (1885), and finally the deeply moving phyrgian *Vexilla regis* (1892). As will be seen, these motets are characterised by a marked predilection for the old church modes, and it is interesting to note that Bruckner succeeded, as he did for instance in the *Os justi*, in adhering strictly to the dictates of the lydian mode without, however, sacrificing his personal style. It is regrettable that these deeply felt choral works are so rarely heard, for although they diverge widely from the Bruckner of the momentous symphonic works they reveal a completely different facet of his character and allow us to sense the depth and purity of his religious feelings.

On a larger scale Bruckner composed five settings of psalms (to German texts) during the course of his life, of which four date from early on and are not to be counted amongst his great works: the 114th and 22nd Psalms of 1852, the 146th Psalm of 1860, and the 112th Psalm of 1863. One setting of a psalm text, however, is among Bruckner's finest religious works. It is the setting of the 150th Psalm of 1892, his last sacred composition and the last but one of all his completed works. It was composed in Vienna where, apart from the *Te Deum*, he composed no other major work of church music. Unfortunately this 150th Psalm is heard relatively rarely, but this apparent neglect is not so much due to lack of musical merit as to the fact that it is overshadowed by the gigantic *Te Deum* of 1883–84. With this *Te Deum* Bruckner created one of his mightiest choral compositions, and it can take its place side by side with the greatest religious works of all time. The shattering impact of the opening, the thematic interrelation of its various parts and the consequent fusion of the individual sections into one integrated whole, and the build-up of the final fugue on the words *In te, Domine, speravi* and *Non confundar in aeternum* are unsurpassed and, one is tempted to say, unsurpassable. Bruckner often introduced short quotations from earlier works of his own into his compositions, and in this respect it is noteworthy that this final climax is introduced by the same theme which brings the Adagio of his 7th Symphony to its culmination, and that the opening motif of the *Te Deum* recurs in the sketches of the unfinished Finale of the 9th Symphony.

In the realm of church music the largest scope is provided by the Mass, and in this form, if one includes the Requiem, Bruckner completed seven compositions. The two earliest, the Mass in C of 1842 and the Mass for Maundy Thursday of 1844, can be disregarded in the present context, despite the 'prophetic' harmonic combinations in the later of the two works. The Requiem in D minor of 1848–49, however, although by no means a work of maturity, is perhaps the first Bruckner composition that deserves to be heard today, for although the influence of the Viennese classics and particularly of Mozart's Requiem is clearly apparent it nevertheless contains passages of pure Bruckner and shows much greater mastery and self-assurance in its conception. Bruckner himself was clearly of the opinion that this Requiem was the best of his earlier works, for much later in life he revised it and presented a copy of it to his friend Franz Bayer (to whom it is dedicated) in Steyr with the laconic comment: 'It isn't bad.' Strangely enough this first major composition is in the key of D minor—the key for which Bruckner had such a predilection throughout his life, the key of his first great Mass and the key of the Symphonies 'No. 0', No. 3 and No. 9. In comparison with this Requiem, his next Mass, the *Missa*

Solemnis in B flat minor of 1854, almost gives the impression of being a retrogression. There is far less individuality in the music, and it cannot be denied that the part writing is at times somewhat awkward, not to say clumsy, which makes performance of the work far more difficult than its musical value would justify.

Now followed a gap of ten years, the years during which Bruckner was completing his studies with Sechter and Kitzler, and at the end of this period he emerged at long last in his full mastery with the three great Masses, composed in the relatively short span of four years: No. 1 in D minor (composed 1864, minor revisions 1876 and 1881–82), No. 2 in E minor (composed 1866, revised 1869, 1876 and 1882), and No. 3 in F minor (composed 1867–68, minor revisions 1876–77, 1881 and between 1890 and 1893). With these three works Bruckner assumed the mantle of Beethoven and Schubert and in many ways the description 'symphonic Masses', which is often attributed to them, is fully justified. Bruckner continues the line from Beethoven's *Missa Solemnis*, and although his harmonic and melodic treatment serves to enhance the words of

St. Florian, the Bruckner Organ in the Stiftskirche

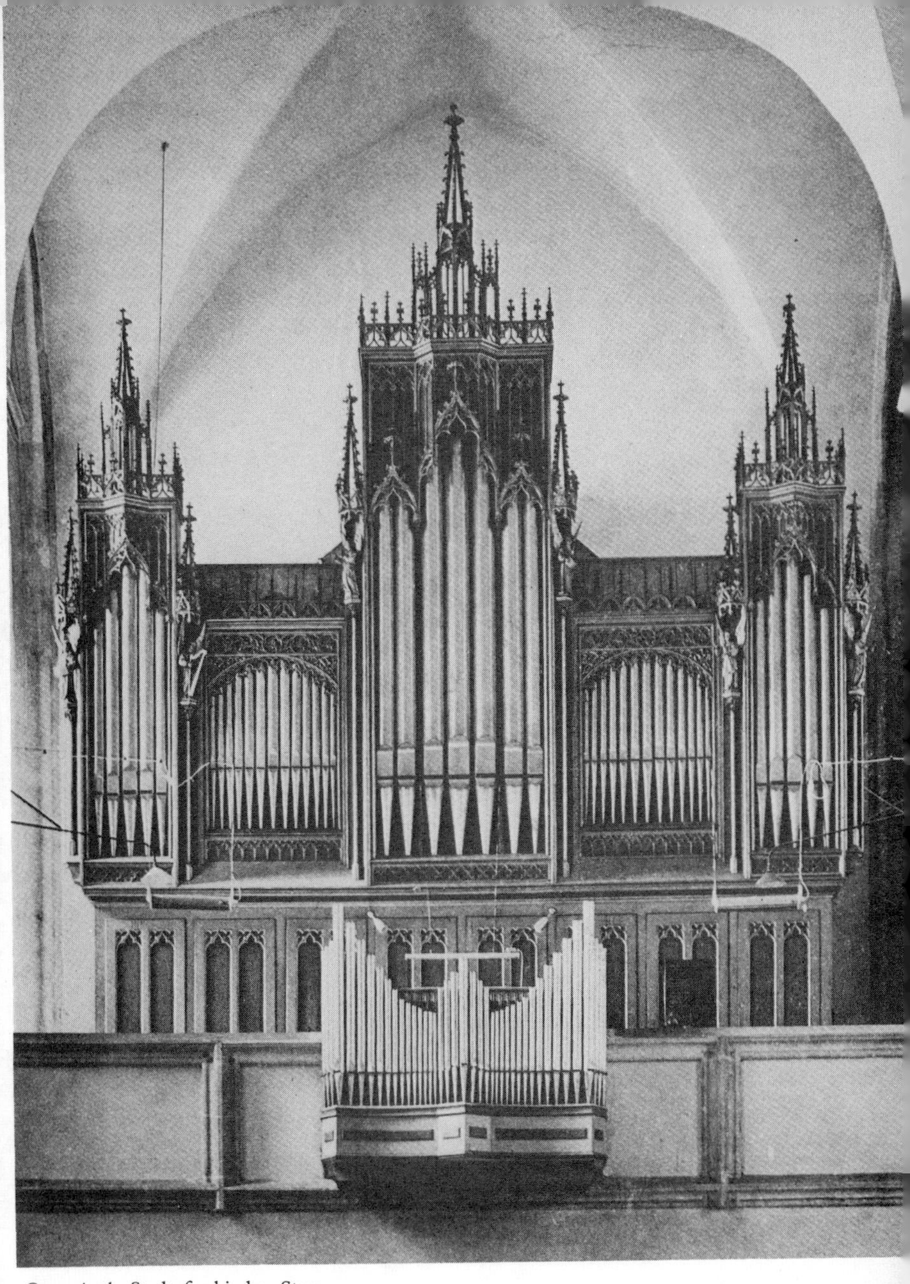

Organ in the Stadtpfarrkirche, *Steyr*

Keyboard and stops of the organ in the old cathedral, Linz

the Mass text, the symphonic element fuses the various contrasting sections of the Mass into one artistic whole. Of the three settings the second, in E minor, occupies a special position. Scored for eight-part chorus, without soli, and wind band accompaniment without organ, it is strongly reminiscent of the great Italian polyphonic era without, however, at any juncture ceasing to be essentially Bruckner. Because of this style it was enthusiastically hailed by the so-called 'Cecilianists'.[1] The Mass had its first performance in the open air, on the occasion of the dedication of the Votive Chapel of the new Linz cathedral, and it has often been assumed that this was the reason for its unique combination of voices and instruments, but this is disproved by a letter which Bruckner wrote to Schiedermayer in 1869, in which he says: 'Unfortunately there is not sufficient space in the choir, but after all we can always perform it in the open.' In any case it is a sublime work in which 'music becomes prayer' (Nowak),

[1] The 'Cecilian Movement' aimed at the reinstatement of Palestrina's *a capella* music instead of the rather worldly church music for choir and instruments that had come into use during the eighteenth century.

The organ in the Stiftskirche, *Kremsmünster*

and in its entire conception it stands in solitary and unique grandeur, not only within the scope of Bruckner's sacred music, but within the whole of Mass composition of the eighteenth and nineteenth centuries. One further point is of interest with regard to these three Masses: in the F minor Mass Bruckner set the entire text, whereas in the two earlier ones, in D minor and E minor, he omitted the words *Gloria in excelsis Deo* and *Credo in unum Deum*, as these are intoned by the priest. This would lead to the assumption that in the two earlier cases he had only the religious service in mind, but when composing the F minor Mass he was beginning to think in terms of concert performance.

Bruckner's entire musical output includes only two works of chamber music: an early String Quartet in C minor of 1862 and the String Quintet in F of 1879 together with the Intermezzo in D minor which Bruckner composed to replace the Scherzo at Hellmesberger's request. The existence of the Quartet was only discovered after the Second World War, and the work had its first performance in 1951. It is in one of Bruckner's exercise books from the days of his studies with Kitzler and constitutes one of his last essays in musical form before he went on to large-scale orchestral composition. The work has a certain charm but must not be rated higher than what it is: an advanced student's exercise. The Quintet is an entirely different matter. This is a work of complete maturity, a worthy successor to the late string quartets of Beethoven, and particularly the Adagio has that glowing richness which is so characteristic of Bruckner. The allegation that the Quintet is in reality a symphony in disguise has already been dealt with[1]; what remains to be said here is that originally Bruckner intended the Scherzo to be the third movement of the work. Later he changed his mind, and before the score went to the engravers he placed the Scherzo second and the Adagio third, thereby creating a much better transition to the Finale.

Immediately after completing the String Quartet Bruckner began composing orchestral music, but his early attempts in this field must also be regarded as 'student works', and although some of them are worthy of the occasional hearing it would go beyond the scope of this book to deal with them in detail. These early orchestral compositions consist of a March in D minor and three Orchestral Pieces of 1862, the Overture in G minor and the Symphony in F minor of 1863, as well as a March in E flat for military band of 1865.[2] In later years Bruckner himself discarded these works, although at the time he appears to have been rather upset when Kitzler referred to the F minor Symphony as 'quite a good piece of homework, but not particularly inspired'. The next symphony, however, the famous 'No. 0' in D minor, is a different matter. Composed or least very fully sketched out in 1863–64, the work was revised and completed in 1869, and when Bruckner sorted through his music in 1895 he did not destroy the score but merely pencilled on it 'not valid' and 'only an attempt'. Naturally, seen through the eyes of the old Bruckner, working on his

[1] See above, p. 75.

[2] The authenticity of the so-called 'Apollo March', as has been mentioned earlier, is exceedingly doubtful.

9th Symphony, this early work must have seemed insignificant and trivial. Nevertheless it represents a great step forward from the F minor Symphony; it is a fully integrated work with great artistic merit of its own and certainly has a place as a sort of 'little brother' to the other nine great symphonies.

We have stressed that Bruckner was first and foremost a symphonist, and it is through the medium of the symphony that most people make their first acquaintance with him. It is not intended to give here a detailed analysis of all nine symphonies,[1] but rather to draw attention to those characteristics which are peculiar to Bruckner's symphonic output, in the hope that this will facilitate an approach to his music and help to reveal something of its astounding emotional range. Here again, as in other matters, Bruckner has suffered from a number of distorting misconceptions.

The first of these is the eternal complaint regarding the length of his symphonies. Certainly, compared with those of his contemporaries, Bruckner's symphonies are long, but it must be borne in mind that he was trying to express in them something entirely new and different. It has been said that whereas Beethoven and Brahms in their symphonies are, as it were, scaling the mountain side, Bruckner stands on the summit and surveys the vast horizons around him. Perhaps this description gives an indication of the 'feel' of Bruckner's music, although it is always impossible to express in words, in concrete terms, the atmosphere of a musical composition. It has also been said that a Bruckner symphony 'encompasses the entire cosmos, from minus infinity to plus infinity', and Halm says that in the opening bars of most of his works it is 'not a symphony which starts, but the very beginning of music itself.'[2] It is obvious that such a conception of timelessness, such breadth of vision, cannot be hurried, and just as Bruckner had the patience to wait until his fortieth year before committing the first of his symphonies to paper, so patience is required of the listener in his approach to a Bruckner symphony.

The second serious misconception is the bracketing together of Bruckner and Mahler. Both composers were Austrian, they each wrote nine symphonies, and all these symphonies are on the lengthy side. There, however, the similarity ends, for the two men were a generation apart, Mahler being thirty-six years younger, and their environments and upbringing were as essentially different as the eras in which they lived and worked. Above all they were of basically different mentalities: Bruckner with his straightforward simplicity never knew a moment's doubt in his fundamental beliefs, whereas Mahler, with his complex and over-civilised personality, hardly knew a moment when he was without doubt. These contrasts make themselves felt in the music of the two

[1] The complex technical questions regarding the 'versions' and the Complete Edition of Bruckner's works are dealt with in Appendix A. See below, p. 170. Excellent and detailed analyses of the symphonies from the harmonic point of view are to be found in Robert Simpson, *The Essence of Bruckner*, Gollancz, 1967. To appreciate these analyses, however, a certain fluency in score-reading and some basic knowledge of harmony are essential.

[2] Halm, *Die Symphonie Anton Bruckners*, Second Edition, Munich, 1923.

men. Bruckner's symphonies all have an underlying calm and progress with inexorable steadiness of pulse from initial problem to ultimate solution; Mahler's symphonies are quite devoid of this calmness and inner balance, and in the end the problem presented at the outset remains unsolved and insoluble.

Finally Bruckner has often been accused of formlessness; all his symphonies, it is said, are in reality one and the same symphony. The second statement is easily disproved if we attempt to single out one Bruckner symphony and analyse it as a 'typical' case. It will soon be found that, having analysed one, it is extremely difficult, not to say impossible, to find a second one which at all conforms to the same pattern. It is true that in comparison with Beethoven there is not so much apparent evidence of development in Bruckner from the first to the

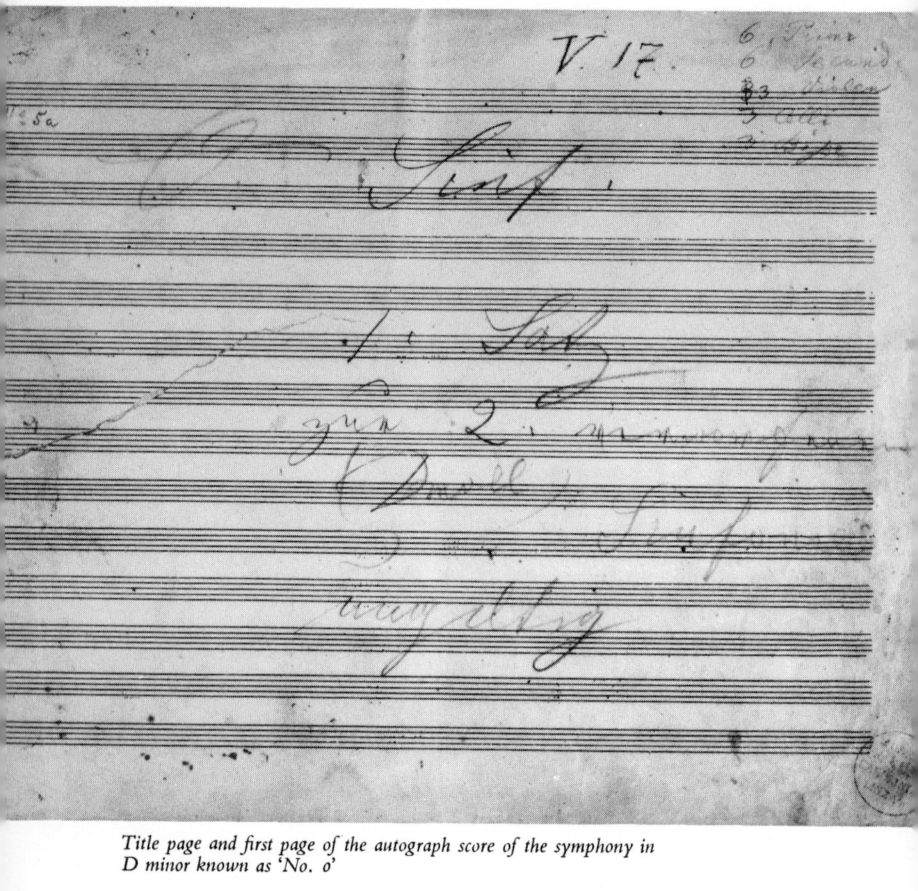

Title page and first page of the autograph score of the symphony in D minor known as 'No. 0'

ninth symphonies, but quite apart from the fact that Bruckner was considerably older and more mature when he began composing symphonies, his development was of a different type. In Beethoven's case we may speak of a linear development, whereas with Bruckner we are faced with a more subtle process: a process of expansion, not only in the mechanical details of orchestration or duration, but also in that indefinable something which might be called spirituality or creative inspiration. To quote Blume once more: 'Bruckner's symphonies give the impression of nine gigantic strides, each more comprehensive, more powerful, more convincing than its predecessor, ever more gripping and intense in the solution of one and the same initial problem.'

As for the accusation of formlessness, this derives to some extent from the effects of the cuts and other alterations made by Bruckner's friends and pupils,

which greatly disturbed the formal structure of his symphonies. Now, however, the original versions are available through the efforts of the International Bruckner Society, and we are able to perceive the clarity and logic of their formal conception. Basically Bruckner adhered to the conventional forms, but he adapted them to his own needs and introduced certain innovations. In his first movements, for example, with the exception of the first movement of No. 5, he dispenses with a slow introduction. Instead they open *pianissimo* on a string tremolo or a characteristic rhythmic figure, so that the entire work seems to emerge out of the void. The thematic material is then presented as in the exposition of the sonata form, except that instead of individual subjects it would be more correct in most cases to speak of groups of themes. Usually these themes are of a strongly contrasting nature, incorporating leaps, usually of the fifth and the octave, as well as scale progressions, thereby furnishing material which lends itself later to the building up of tension and antithesis in the development sections. In the second group the themes often appear simultaneously, and the first outstanding example of this is to be found in the opening movement of No. 3 (bars 101 ff.) where the second violins play their theme in the famous 'Bruckner rhythm'[1] whilst the violas sing a counter-melody. There is an even more noticeable instance in the Finale of the same symphony (bars 65ff.) where the violins have a rather gay, dancelike tune against the background of a sombre chorale in the brass. A novelty with Bruckner is the great importance given to the third subject. This usually occurs near the end of the exposition and is sometimes a completely new theme, sometimes closely related to earlier material. The idea of such a third or '*coda*' subject was not new—Beethoven had already introduced it in his *Eroica*—but never before had it been given such prominence. The exposition of all Bruckner's first movements and most of his Finales is completed in this way. Basically all these movements have the characteristics of sonata form, and for the sake of convenience the terminology normally associated with this form is here adhered to. However, it must be pointed out that Bruckner was never a classical 'formalist'. Sonata form as it had come down to him from the Viennese classics and especially Beethoven and Schubert (and of these two composers it was particularly the former's Ninth and the latter's 'Great C major' which exerted strong influence on him) was for him a mere starting point, which he filled out, moulded and fashioned to suit his own particular requirements. Thus the recapitulation with Bruckner is never a schematic repetition, but a recurrence of the original material on a far higher plane. In the course of the development the thematic material undergoes a type of metamorphosis, the harmonic structure moves through vast changes and brings entirely new tensions. If a simile is permitted, one might perhaps liken the three sections customarily known as exposition, development and recapitulation in Bruckner's sonata-type movements to the three metamorphic stages of caterpillar, chrysalis and butterfly. A further characteristic to be noted in Bruckner's first movements

[1] See note p. 59.

First two pages of the autograph score of Symphony No. 3, the so-called Wagner Symphony'

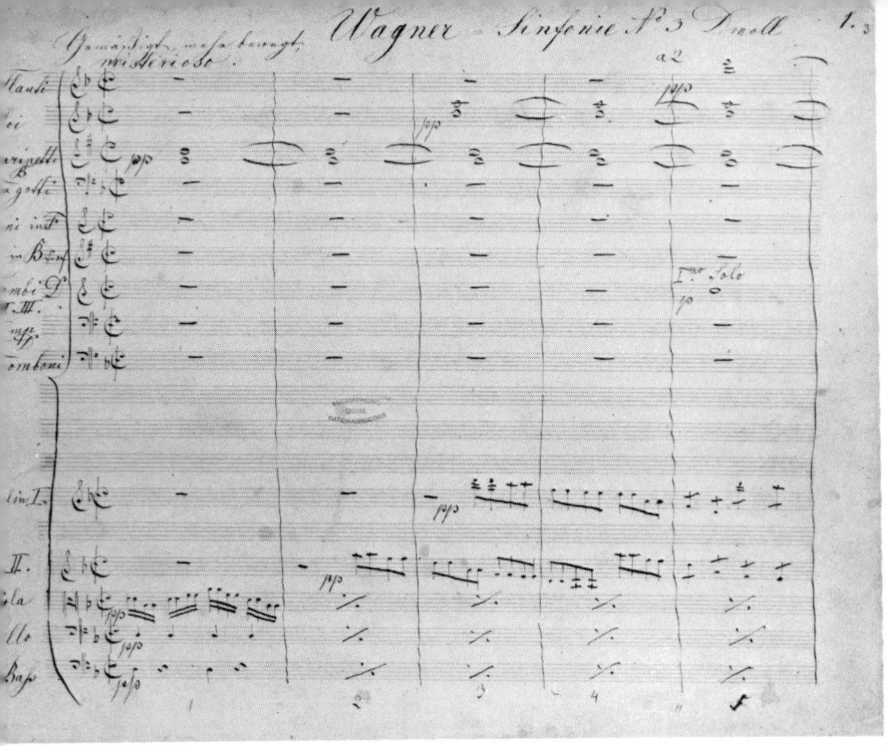
Wagner – Sinfonie No 3 D moll
misterioso
a 2
Imo Solo

A page (p. 72 of the printed score as published in the Complete Edition) of the Te Deum *at the words* 'Non confundar', *with the theme which is also of paramount importance in the Adagio of Symphony No. 7*

and in his Finales is the enormous extension of the *coda*. This is no longer an innocuous little tail-section to bring the movement to a close but a mighty summing-up of all that has gone before. In the case of the first movements, these come to their conclusion in an overwhelming restatement of the main subject, with the exception of the first movement of No. 8 in its second version, which finishes *pianissimo*, and in the Finales also it is usually the main subject of the first movement which, in conjunction with the actual Finale theme, brings the whole symphony to a glorious conclusion, closing the circle and thematically joining the very end of the symphony to its very beginning. In the Finale of No. 8 Bruckner surpassed himself by superimposing the main themes of all four movements in one gigantic climax, thereby not only giving the most complete summing-up of the entire symphonic event, but also demonstrating the close relationship between what to the listener might have appeared to be four unconnected ideas. Through this extension of the *coda*, however, the basic subdivision into three major sections which is inherent in music to such a large degree became endangered. Bruckner countered this by introducing a kind of telescopic effect into his great outer movements, fusing 'development' and 'recapitulation' and thereby re-establishing the tripartite structure. In the earlier symphonies this is achieved by shifting the climax of the development to the very end of the section, so that the culmination of the development coincides with the recapitulation of the first subject. Examples are to be found in the first movements of No. 3, bars 341 ff., No. 5, bars 363 ff., and No. 6, bars 209 ff. By No. 9 this telescoping or contraction has resulted in a true fusion so that the original basic sections of the sonata form can no longer be distinguished. Development and recapitulation have become one inseparable entity, and the best way of approaching the form of this first movement is the subdivision suggested by Robert Simpson into statement, expanded counterstatement and coda.

A special word must be said about the Finale of No. 5, as this movement is unique not only in Bruckner's work, but in the whole realm of symphonic music. It combines perfect mastery of formal conception and contrapuntal craftsmanship with profound inspiration and broad vision. In it two forms are fused into one: the sonata form and the double fugue, and despite their essential difference the fusion is perfect. For the benefit of those readers who may wish to go into the structure of this particular movement more deeply, the following brief analysis may be of interest.

The movement opens with a slow introduction similar to that of the first movement, but in this instance it also incorporates the 'motto' theme of the entire movement (the very opening of the first fugue subject) as well as reminiscences of the first and second movements. The movement proper (*Allegro moderato*), after the 'motto' has been stated once again, begins with the first sonata subject which is also the first fugue subject, and this is treated in the way of a strict fugal exposition (bars 31–66). Then follows the second sonata group of subjects which receives no fugal treatment (bars 67–136), and the third or 'coda' group (bars 137–174) is based on the 'motto', both in its original rhythm and in augmentation. This third group ends on a great chorale played by all the brass (bar 175), and the 'exposition' of the sonata form comes to a conclusion at bar 210. The 'development' begins with a restatement of the first four bars of the chorale melody, which now turns out to be the second fugue subject and is also treated in the way of a fugal exposition (bars 223–269). Then follows a long development section (bars 270–373) in which both fugue subjects are freely interwoven in their original forms as well as in inversion. The 'recapitulation' begins at bar 374, but this time both fugue subjects are to be heard simultaneously, and they are succeeded (bar 398) by a restatement of the (non-fugal) second thematic group. As in the exposition, the third group with the 'motto' theme follows (bar 460) which now also comprises the

Page from the first printed score of Symphony No. 7 with the dedication to the King of Bavaria

Seiner Majestät

dem Könige

LUDWIG II.

von Bayern

in tiefster Ehrfurcht

gewidmet.

main subject of the first movement. This leads to the *coda* (bars 496 ff.), which opens on a statement of the 'motto' in the low strings and soon combines this 'motto' with the first movement subject. The climax of the whole movement sets in with a further statement in the full orchestra of the 'motto', in augmentation and both in its original form and its inversion (bars 564–582), and the culmination is reached when the brass blazes forth the chorale in augmentation (bar 583) over the rhythmic background of the 'motto'. The symphony comes to its conclusion on the principal subject of the first movement.

Although the above reduces the complex structure of the movement to its barest essentials and omits all reference to harmonic texture, it may serve to give some small insight into the enormous complexity of the formal problem confronting Bruckner in this fusing of two opposed entities, and the masterly way in which he solved this problem. A symphonic *tour de force* indeed, and no wonder that he was wont to refer to this 5th Symphony as the 'Fantastic'. As far as one can gather from the existing sketches, the Finale of the 9th Symphony would have been somewhat similar in construction had he been permitted to complete it. This movement was planned without a slow introduction, but the incisive rhythm of the opening theme, the great chorale which was to become the crowning glory of the epilogue, and the inclusion of a fugal exposition in the course of the movement, point towards this assumption. In these sketches, incidentally, Bruckner quotes the opening figuration of his *Te Deum*; he even wrote the words *Te Deum* above the score. This has led certain musicians to believe that Bruckner intended to compose a transitional passage to enable the *Te Deum* to be played as a Finale should he die before the completion of the composition. This supposition, however, is surely erroneous, for Bruckner was fond of quoting his own compositions in later works. The Adagio of No. 9 contains references to the D minor Mass as well as to Nos. 7 and 8; there is a quotation from the *Benedictus* of the F minor Mass in the second movement of No. 2, and the main theme of No. 5 is quoted in the Trio of the Scherzo of No. 6; the use of the motif from the Adagio of No. 7 in the *Te Deum* has already been mentioned. Besides, Bruckner was well aware that this symphony would be his last. Having dedicated No. 7 to the King of Bavaria and No. 8 to the Emperor of Austria, he intended No. 9 to be dedicated 'To my dear Lord', as he told Dr. Heller who was treating him at the time. So what could be more natural than for him to include in its Finale a musical allusion to one of his greatest sacred works whose words, *Te Deum laudamus*, were the lodestar by which he guided his entire life.

The formal structure of Bruckner's Adagios, the second movement in all symphonies[1] up to No. 7 and the third movement in Nos. 8 and 9, is a more difficult matter. All his Adagios are characterised by having two groups of themes, of which the second is usually the more flowing, often being described by Bruckner himself in his scores as *Gesangsthema* or *Gesangsperiode*, and some of these slow movements also have a third group in analogy with the outer

[1] In No. 2 and No. 4 the slow movements are marked Andante, but the principles under discussion still apply to them.

Last two pages of the printed score of Symphony No. 8 (as published in the Complete Edition) superimposing the main themes of all four movements

riten.
(a 2)
1.2.
Fl.
3.
a 2
1.2.
Ob.
3.
1.2. in B
Klar.
3. in B
Fag. 1.2
K.-Fag.
(a 2)
1.2. in F
Hrn.
3.4. in B
Ten.-Tb.
1.2 in B
a 2
B.-Tb.
1.2 in F
1. in F
Tromp.
2.3. in C
(a 2)
A.T.
Pos.
B.
K.-Btb.
Pk.
riten.
Viol. 1
Viol. 2
Vla.
Vc.
Kb.
riten.

An advertisement issued by the Viennese publisher Gutmann, quoting excerpts of press notices relating to the 7th Symphony

Verlag der kais. kön. Hof-Musikalien-Handlung

Albert J. Gutmann in Wien.

Siebente Symphonie (E-dur)

von

Anton Bruckner.

Dieses Werk wurde mit ausserordentlichem Erfolge aufgeführt: in Leipzig (Capellmeister Nikisch), München (Hof-Capellmeister Levi), Karlsruhe (beim Musikfeste des Deutschen Tonkünstler-Vereins, Dirigent Hof-Capellmeister Felix Mottl), Köln (Capellmeister Dr. Wüllner), Hamburg (Capellmeister Bernuth), Graz (Capellmeister Muck), Wien durch die **„Philharmoniker“** unter Hof-Capellmeister Hanns Richter's Leitung.

Kernsprüche aus kritischen Referaten.

Das Werk fordert die höchste Bewunderung heraus.
„Leipziger Nachrichten“ vom 1. Januar 1885. **Bernhard Vogel.**

Bruckner ist ein Genie, das sich an Beethoven herangebildet hat und in der That Züge zeigt, die Beethoven's würdig wären.
Referat über das Karlsruher Musikfest des Deutschen Musikvereins.
„Frankfurter Zeitung“ vom 1. Juni 1885.

Das ist endlich einmal ein Tondichter, welcher nicht mit sorgsamer Klügelei kleine und nichtige Themen zu etwas Grossem zu erheben sich abmüht, sondern der schon ursprünglich wahrhaft gross empfindet.
Münchener „Neueste Nachrichten“ vom 12. März 1885.

Die ersten drei Sätze sind hochbedeutend, die Themata des Adagio von ergreifender Schönheit, der Aufbau imposant. Durch das Ganze geht ein grosser Zug.
Berliner „Tageblatt“ vom 13. März 1885.
Dr. Paul Marsop.
(Bericht über die Münchener Aufführung, mitgetheilt durch H. Ehrlich.)

Wie wohl thut es, einmal wieder einem im besten Sinne naiven Tondichter zu begegnen, der nicht grübelt, sondern aus innerstem Bedürfnisse schafft.
„Deutsche Zeitung“ vom 25. März 1886. **Dr. Theodor Helm.**

Wie die früheren symphonischen Arbeiten dieses Componisten ist auch sein neues Werk durch wahrhaft schöpferische Kraft ausgezeichnet.
„Morgen-Post“ vom 23. März 1886. **Dr. Oskar Berggruen.**

Die neueste Symphonie ist von einer Macht der Empfindung, wie sie nur den grössten unserer deutschen Tondichter nachgerühmt werden kann.
„Neues Wiener Tagblatt“ vom 30. März 1886. **W. Frey.**

So steht die 7. Bruckner'sche Symphonie als ein unvergängliches Tonbauwerk vor uns. Die Zeit ist ganz nahe, in welcher die symphonischen Werke Bruckner's die Programme aller Concerte erfüllen und in das Herz aller Musikmenschen eindringen werden. Vorurtheil und Indolenz können quälen, aber niemals hindern
„Wr. Abendpost“ vom 27. März 1886. **Dr. Hans Paumgartner.**

Ich bekenne unumwunden, dass ich über Bruckner's Symphonie kaum ganz gerecht urtheilen könnte, so antipathisch berührt mich diese Musik, so unnatürlich aufgeblasen, krankhaft und verderblich erscheint sie mir.
„Neue Freie Presse“ vom 30. März 1886. **Dr. Eduard Hanslick.**

Bruckner componirt wie ein Betrunkener.
„Wr. Allgemeine Zeitung“. **Gustav Doempke.**

Entry in Bruckner's diary giving details of the original scores contained in a 'sealed parcel'

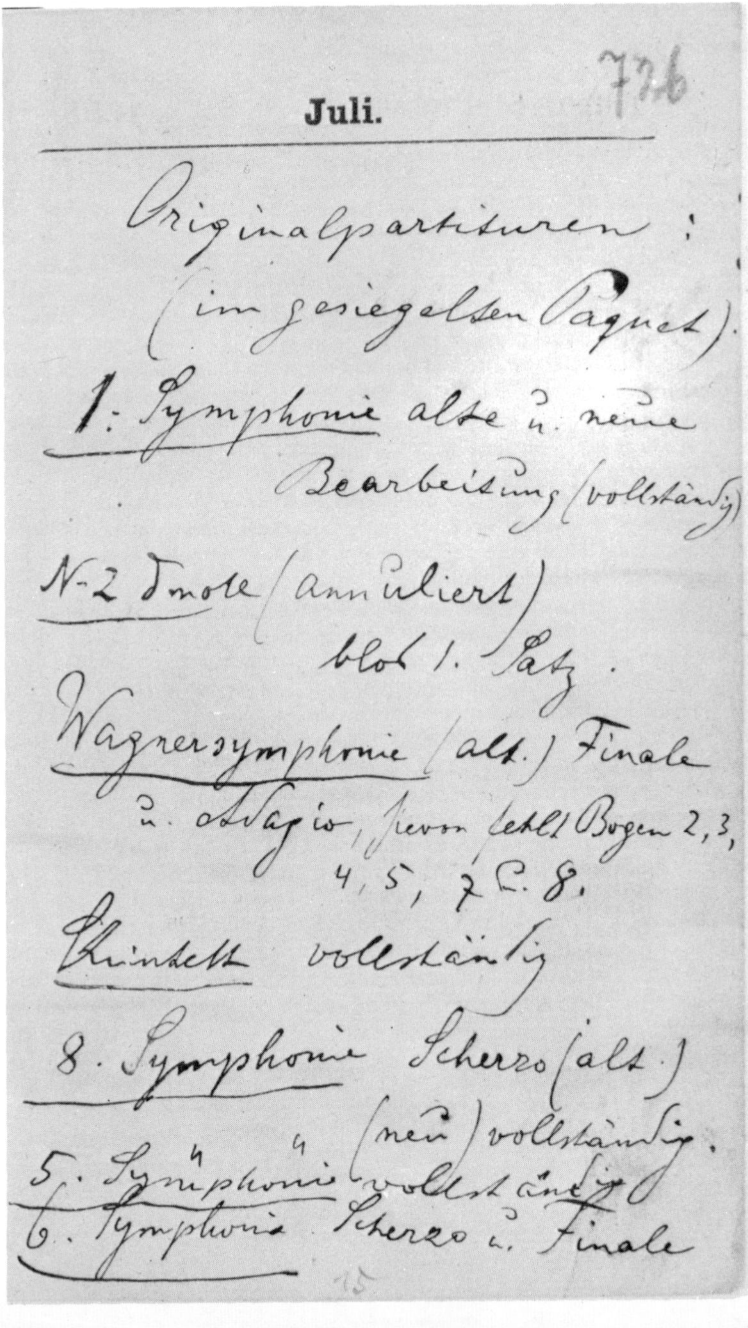
Juli.

726

Originalpartituren:
(im gesiegelten Paquet).
1. Symphonie alte u. neue
Bearbeitung (vollständig)
N-2 Cmoll (annulliert)
blos 1. Satz.
Wagnersymphonie (alt.) Finale
u. Adagio, hievon fehlt Bogen 2, 3,
4, 5, 7 u. 8.
Quintett vollständig
8. Symphonie Scherzo (alt.)
(neu) vollständig.
5. Symphonie vollständig
6. Symphonie Scherzo u. Finale

movements. The attempt has been made to assign definite formal types to these Adagios, but with the exception of that of No. 6, which is a relatively clear-cut sonata form in the Brucknerian sense, this is virtually impossible, as in most of them traces of sonata, rondo and even variation form can be discovered. One thing that stands out quite clearly is the influence of the Adagio of Beethoven's 9th Symphony, most markedly so in the Adagios of Bruckner's last three symphonies. Rather than get involved in a lengthy discussion of the academic side of this problem, it will be more useful here to regard these Adagios in a purely musical light, in the effect which they have upon the listener. Here it must be said first and foremost that no other composer since Beethoven had been able to concieve Adagios on such a vast scale which yet never lose their inner cohesion and their poignancy. On this large canvas the themes appear to develop, to grow, to blossom forth. In this context Bruckner's climatic treatment, which does not only apply to the Adagios, is of interest. He builds up his climaxes by the use of sequential repetitions, i.e. the same musical phrase repeated several times, but each time one or more tones higher, and for this he has been much criticised. In German musical parlance such sequences are known as *Schusterflecke* (literally 'cobbler's patches') and are considered a stop-gap measure for when the flow of inspiration dries up. In Bruckner's case, however, their use is fully justified, as they spring from his innermost self. They do not stem from any lack of ideas; they are his own way of building up those towering heights to which his music rises in a series of symphonic waves. Furthermore it is essential to realise that all Bruckner's movements have only one true climax. In fact some authorities go so far as to say that there is only one true climax in each entire symphony, a point of view which certainly has much to support it. But within the movement Bruckner has a way of building up *towards* a climax, and then, just as one approaches the peak, the 'wave' glides past without breaking, the music slips into a quieter flow, and the next build-up commences. Occasionally Bruckner repeats this process two or three times, and the tension and expectation of release build up to an incredible degree until the last great 'wave' finally leads to the actual climax, which comes with such a shattering impact as to be almost unbearable. Perhaps the greatest examples of this treatment are to be found in the Adagios of No. 7 at bar 177 and No. 8 at bar 253. This climax normally heralds the beginning of the *coda*, which is usually in the nature of a quiet epilogue, though in the Adagio of No. 7 it marks the beginning of the funeral music for Wagner.

The Scherzi of the symphonies are, on the whole, much more straightforward, and it is in these movements that the Austrian element in Bruckner is most pronounced. Especially in the earlier symphonies the main section of the Scherzo is unmistakably a peasant dance, and the Trio often has the character of a quiet *Ländler*. In the case of the Scherzo of No. 4 with its horn calls, the description 'Hunting Scherzo' really says everything, and although in the four following symphonies the Scherzi take on a more symphonic aspect, their origin in the dances of Upper Austria is still quite obvious. The great exception is the Scherzo of No. 9, for here Bruckner enters an entirely new world. The main section of the Scherzo, if it can still be called a dance, is more in the nature of a giants' dance for it has some almost terrifying moments. Nor is this impression relieved by the Trio, the swiftest movement which Bruckner ever composed, for instead of bringing the customary relaxation of tension it provides a sort of supernatural vision of shadowy shapes flitting by. With regard to the Austrian dance element in the majority of the Scherzi, an element which quite likely reflects back to Bruckner's young days when he played the fiddle at village dances, it must be stressed that these dance melodies fit into the general framework of the symphonies with complete naturalness.

Page from the first printed score of Symphony No. 8 with the dedication to the Emperor of Austria

Seiner

K. u. K. Apostolischen Majestät

FRANZ JOSEF I.

Kaiser von Oesterreich

und Apostolischer König von Ungarn etc. etc.

in tiefster Ehrfurcht

Anton Bruckner.

The 'Chorale' climax, Finale of Symphony No. 5 (p. 175 of the printed score as published in the Complete Edition)

They are an integral part of the flow of the music, and one never has the impression of an artificial superimposition for the sake of nationalistic colouring—an impression which one cannot quite escape at times in the case of Mahler. Nor does Bruckner ever resort to any unusual instruments such as mandolines, cowbells or alphorns, to produce special effects or local colouring as some other composers have done. With Bruckner all that is characteristic lies in the melodic line, the rhythm and the harmonic structure, and he achieves his end with a perfectly conventional orchestral complement. As a rule both the Scherzo and its Trio are in ternary form with one main theme each, which is presented, developed and then recapitulated in a very free way. The notable exception is No. 5, where the main Scherzo section is in reality a sonata form in miniature.

Perhaps one further aspect could be examined at this juncture in connection with Bruckner's method of composition: his great predelection for the contrapuntal devices of inversion, augmentation and diminution. No doubt they find their origin in his training and activities as an organist, but it is in his symphonic writing that they come so noticeably to the fore. There is hardly a theme throughout his symphonies which he does not invert (i.e. where he replaces each ascending interval by the corresponding descending one and *vice versa*), and in many cases his contrapuntal mastery is a source of never ending astonishment and admiration—to find that a theme and its inversion can be played simultaneously, or that the inversion of the theme is a perfect counterpoint to the theme in its original form, but in augmentation. It is very strange, however, that despite this obvious facility in the contrapuntal treatment of his themes Bruckner never makes use of that other device known as the 'crab': his themes never appear in the retrograde form (i.e. commencing with the last note and then bringing all the intervals of the theme in reverse order), and one might almost be led to assume that this particular contrapuntal device was incompatible with the essential forward flow and surge of his music and of his personal outlook.

Contrary to a common misconception, Bruckner's orchestra is by no means bloated. In fact, for the most part, the instrumental forces which he utilises are slightly smaller than those required for a Brahms symphony. The first six symphonies are scored at the most for double woodwind, four horns, three trumpets, three trombones and tuba, timpani and strings, and it is only in No. 7 that he introduces the quartet of Wagner tubas. Only in Nos. 8 and No. 9 does he employ triple woodwind, and in these symphonies the number of horns is also increased to eight, with the third and fourth pairs doubling on Wagner tubas. The harp only occurs in No. 8, and Nos. 7 and 8 alone contain any percussion instruments apart from the timpani: one cymbal clash in the Adagio of No. 8 and the dubious[1] percussion entry in the Adagio of No. 7. It is especially remarkable that Bruckner, reputedly so Wagnerian in his orchestral treatment, never uses piccolo, cor anglais or bass clarinet, and the double bassoon only occurs in one or two isolated instances in his symphonies.

[1] See below, p. 177.

It is the way Bruckner uses his orchestral forces which gives the impression that it must be a gigantic apparatus which he employs.

In contrast to Wagner, who considered music to be the 'art of transition', Bruckner orchestrated in terms of blocks of sound, and it frequently happens that a *pianissimo* section scored for strings is interrupted by a *fortissimo* entry of the entire brass complement. These sudden changes of texture are characteristic of Bruckner, and one is irresistibly reminded of the sound produced by a great organ when suddenly all the stops are pulled or when the organist changes from one manual to another. It is this 'block' orchestration and the sharp dividing lines which ensue taken in conjunction with the pauses Bruckner is wont to make at the end of a section, which have earned him the reputation of being unable to write a smooth transition. But wherever these sharp divides occur, it is by no means through inability to effect a transition. From the most purely practical point of view these divisions serve the very necessary purpose of preserving clarity of form, for Bruckner's symphonic movements are so extended that without these clear dividing lines the listener could easily become lost. The primary reason, however, for these pauses and interruptions lies in Bruckner's unique mode of expression. He himself made this abundantly clear in his simple way when, in reply to the young Nikisch's comment on the many rests in the 2nd Symphony, he said, 'But look, if I have something important to say I must first take a deep breath!' It is true that the pauses pose a difficult problem for the conductor, but in a good and meaningful interpretation their essential rightness and especially their metrical significance in the formal design become fully apparent, and in such a performance these silences can become most poignantly eloquent. Take, for example, the general pause in bar 212 of the Finale of No. 7. Here an enormous climax is reached by the full orchestra on a *unisono* passage based on the principal theme, then there is utter silence, and gently the strings enter *pianissimo* with the chorale-like second subject. On the other hand there are many instances of the most superb transitions to be found in Bruckner's music, transitions in which he joins one section to another with such perfect smoothness that a newcomer to his symphonies would be forgiven for not even noticing that a new section had started. Clear examples of such transitions are to be found in the first movement of No. 4, bars 333–364, where an augmentation of the second subject leads to the recapitulation; in the first movement of No. 6, bars 195–209, where the climax of the development coincides with the recapitulation of the first subject; and in many places in his slow movements. Proof enough, at any rate, that Bruckner was not prevented from writing transitions by lack of skill or inspiration!

Among the features which are so typical of Bruckner the great unisons and the incorporation of chorales must be mentioned. *Unisono* passages in the full orchestra occur in almost all his symphonies and always have a climactic effect. One example, in the Finale of No. 7, has already been cited, and such passages are so frequent that it is impossible to mention them all. Two outstanding instances, however, are the first statement of the principal theme in the Finale

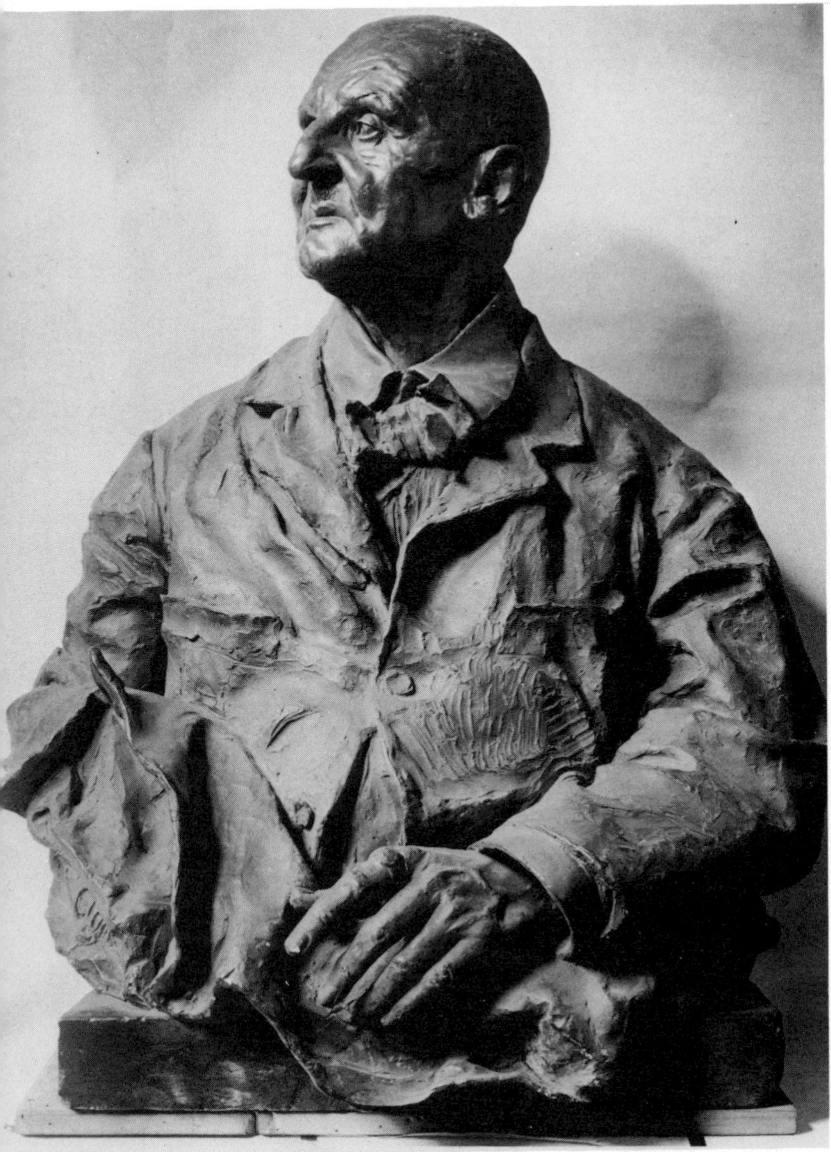

Anton Bruckner. Bust by Viktor Tilgner

Gustav Mahler

of No. 4, bars 43–49, and perhaps that supreme moment of all, the main subject of the first movement of No. 9, bars 63–70, when the entire orchestra in mighty unison crashes down in its gigantic octave leaps. The effect of these unisons is cataclysmic, and the apparent simplicity of means only serves to increase the elemental impact. Similarly Bruckner achieves moments of utter sublimity with his chorales, in connection with which it must be said that they are never existing chorales of which Bruckner made use (as many other composers before and since his day have done), but always chorale-like melodies of his own invention. At times he himself wrote the word *Choral* above the bars in question (No. 3, first movement; No. 5, Finale), but they occur as such in almost every one of his symphonies. At times they appear in the full splendour of concerted brass, in which case the chorale always marks a special climax, but at others they form part of the second thematic group and are usually allocated to the strings playing *pianissimo*, providing moments of repose, of peace and meditation which cannot fail to move the listener.

One final point must be made which is rarely given sufficient prominence and which is yet so important in Bruckner's symphonies, as it is one of the most vital factors for cohesion within their immense span. This is the very strong thematic relationship which exists between the various movements of each symphony. In some cases this cohesion is achieved by direct quotation of thematic material from earlier movements. In the brief analysis of the Finale of No. 5 such quotations, from the first and second movements, have already been mentioned, and it has been seen that almost invariably the Finale of a Bruckner symphony culminates with a restatement of the principal subject of the first movement. Another instance is the Finale of No. 4 where the horn call of the Scherzo recurs shortly before the statement of the main theme, bars 28–42, and the first climax after the exposition of the principal subject brings in the main theme of the first movement, bars 79–89. However, in many cases the thematic connections are far more subtle, and in all probability many listeners feel the resultant cohesion subconsciously without ever being aware of the reason for it. Such connections are so frequent in Bruckner's symphonies as to have prompted some authorities to go so far as to say that they are virtually monothematic. Without going to such extremes it may be of interest to cite just four examples: in No. 4 the intervals of the opening horn theme, the fall and rise of a fifth, are duplicated exactly in the first three notes of the opening 'cello melody of the slow movement; in No. 5 the first four bars of the Adagio are reproduced note by note in the first eight bars of the Scherzo, though at a much faster pace; in No. 6 the plaintive little oboe melody at the beginning of the slow movement, bars 5–6, in the same rhythmic pattern and almost identical notes but in an entirely different context, forms part of the Finale, bars 150–151; and lastly there can be no mistaking the first subject of the Finale of No. 7 as being a rhythmic variant of the principal theme of the first movement. These interrelations, moreover, go further than simply securing the inner cohesion of his symphonic structures. They form part of that mysterious process of metamorphosis which has been mentioned earlier in connection with formal

Page from the autograph sketches for the unfinished Finale of Symphony No. 9

structure, and which is so essentially Bruckner's own.

In conclusion it may be said that Bruckner's musical roots reach back to Palestrina, to Bach, to Beethoven and Schubert, and that his formal outlook is fashioned by the baroque of St. Florian and by the gothic of the *Stadtpfarrkiche* in Steyr and later of the *Stephansdom* in Vienna. His music contains passages of the deepest mysticism, yet he was no mystic. His symphonies contain melodies which take us back to the folksong and folk dances of Upper Austria, yet Bruckner was no peasant simpleton. In every bar of his music he strives towards his 'dear Lord', searches for him in the expanse of the universe and in the narrow confines of his native countryside. Bruckner has been called *der Musikant Gottes*, 'God's own musician', and it has been said that each of his symphonies is in reality one gigantic arch which starts on earth in the midst of suffering humanity, sweeps up towards the heavens to the very Throne of Grace, and returns to earth with a message of peace. Alfred Orel wrote that 'Bruckner has freed the orchestral sound of Wagner from the shackles of materialism', and Bruckner himself said that his symphonies as he had written them were meant for 'times to come'. Max Auer, in his address on the occasion of the fiftieth anniversary of Bruckner's death, in 1946, said:

> 'The time is at hand of which Ernst Kurth spoke when he said: "Bruckner will be ready for the world when the world has to flee to him for refuge." Bruckner may be the lay apostle who with his work, which projects the divine idea into the world in its purest form, may touch the hearts of those whose ears are closed to the preaching of the churches. He can become the mediator leading from materialism to spirituality, from disbelief to true religion.'

The Problem of the Versions

The question of the various 'versions' of Bruckner's symphonies is complex and confusing. This confusion arises in the first place from Bruckner's own repeated revisions and in the second place from the alterations made by well-meaning friends, and it is increased still further by the diverging opinions of several authorities as to what constitutes a new version. Bruckner frequently took out the score of one or other of his completed symphonies and made some minor adjustments, and if each adjustment were to be considered to constitute a new 'version', the number of different versions in existence of each symphony would indeed be countless. It is therefore necessary to define certain groupings, and to consider as a new version only a form of the particular symphony which differs decisively from its predecessors, in order to reduce the problem to manageable proportions. In the following list the nine major symphonies, Nos. 1–9, are treated individually, showing the various versions as they came about, without going into such detail as would result in obscuring the very issue which it is meant to clarify[1].

No. 1 in C minor

LINZ VERSION: Composed 1865–66; minor additions and alterations in 1868 (for the first performance), 1877, and 1884 (Adagio).

VIENNA VERSION: Thorough revision of the entire score 1890–91.

First Performance:	9 May 1868, Linz, under Bruckner (Linz Version.)
	13 December 1891, Vienna, under Richter (Vienna Version)
First Publication:	1893, by Jos. Eberle & Co.

No. 2 in C minor

VERSION I: Composed 1871–72; minor revision in 1873 (for the first performance)

[1] This problem is elucidated in an exemplary manner in a series of five articles by Deryck Cooke, entitled 'The Bruckner Problem Simplified', in the *Musical Times* (Jan., Feb., Apr., May, and Aug. 1969).

VERSION II: Alterations, cuts etc. in 1876–77 with minor alterations in 1879.

First Performance:	26 October 1873, Vienna, under Bruckner (Version I) 20 February 1876, Vienna, under Bruckner (Version II)
First Publication:	1892, by Jos. Eberle & Co.

No. 3 in D minor

VERSION I: Composed 1873; 'considerably improved' (Bruckner) in 1874.

VERSION II: Thorough revision (excision of Wagner quotations) 1876–77 with further minor amendments in 1878.

VERSION III: Thorough revision 1888–89.

First Performance:	16 December 1877, Vienna, under Bruckner (Version II) 21 December 1890, Vienna, under Richter (Version III)
First Publication:	1878, by Th. Rättig (Bussjäger & Rättig) (Version II) 1890, by Th. Rättig (Version III)

No. 4 in *E flat, 'Romantic'*

VERSION I: Composed 1874.

VERSION II: Thorough revision of the entire score 1878 including composition of new Scherzo; new Finale in 1879–80; minor alterations in 1881 and about 1886.

VERSION III[1]: Major alterations and excisions, due mainly to Ferdinand Löwe, in 1887–88. Although Bruckner must have seen these alterations, he did not sign or initial them (see pp. 91–93.)

First Performance:	20 February 1881, Vienna, under Richter (Version II) 22 January 1888, Vienna, under Richter (Version III)
First Publication:	1890, by Albert Gutmann (Version III)

No. 5 in B flat

Only one version, composed 1875–76 with minor revisions 1877–78.

First Performance:	8 April 1894, Graz, under Franz Schalk (in a version recomposed by Schalk without Bruckner's consent or knowledge)
First Publication:	1896, by Ludwig Doblinger

No. 6 in A

Only one version, composed 1879–81.

First Performance:	11 February 1883, Vienna, under Jahn (2nd and 3rd movements) 26 February 1899, Vienna, under Mahler (with major cuts) 14 March 1901, Stuttgart, under Pohlig (complete)
First Publication:	1899, by Ludwig Doblinger

No. 7 in E

Only one version, composed 1881–83.

[1] Although called here 'Version III' for the sake of clarity, this version cannot be said to constitute an 'original' Bruckner version.

First Performance: 30 December 1884, Leipzig, under Nikisch
First Publication: 1885, by Albert Gutmann

No. 8 in C minor

VERSION I: Composed 1884–87.

VERSION II: Thorough revision of the entire score 1889–90: augmented orchestration and new Trio, major excisions, and new ending of first movement.

First Performance: 18 December 1892, Vienna, under Richter (Version II)
First Publication: 1892, by Robert Lienau (Schlesinger) (Version II)

No. 9 in D minor

One version only. First three movements composed 1891–94, but sketches go back to 1887; Sketches for Finale from 1894 until his death in 1896.

First Performance: 11 February 1903, Vienna, under Löwe (in a version recomposed by Löwe after Bruckner's death.)
First Publication: 1903, by Universal Edition

It must be stressed that none of the 'first publications' listed above represented Bruckner's own will. Allusion has already been made to the well-meaning but (as can now be seen quite clearly) misguided friends and pupils, foremost among them Ferdinand Löwe and Franz Schalk, who considered it necessary to assist Bruckner's cause by 'editing' his scores, and it is in these edited forms that they were first published. In some cases the alterations were of a comparatively minor nature, but in others the changes in orchestration and the excisions, without in the least casting aspersions on the integrity of the editors' intentions, can only be said to have resulted in mutilation. This applies in particular to No. 4, No. 5 and No. 9. In No. 4 and No. 5 large-scale cuts entirely destroyed Bruckner's formal balance, and the far-reaching changes in orchestration in No. 5 and No. 9 altered the sound of these works beyond recognition.

In 1927 the International Bruckner Society (I.B.S.) was founded in Leipzig, and Professor Max Auer became its first president. Its general aim was the propagation of Bruckner's music both at home and abroad, but its most important function was to be the publication of his works in their original form. Needless to say, this project at first met with a certain amount of scepticism and opposition, but on 2 April 1932 came the turning point. On that date Siegmund von Hausegger, conducting the Munich Philharmonic Orchestra, played what had hitherto been the only known version of the Symphony No. 9 and followed it with the original version, and Auer writes that this juxtaposition had the effect of 'a huge painting being freed from the dust of centuries, so that outlines which formerly had been only dimly discernible suddenly became clearly visible, and all colours acquired a luminosity comparable to an old church window'. The publication of the Complete Edition of Bruckner's works in their original form was entrusted to Dr. Robert Haas who, together with

Alfred Orel, devoted all his time and energy to this herculean task until 1945 when he was succeeded by Professor Leopold Nowak.

It took some time for these original versions to establish themselves, for time-honoured usage is difficult to eradicate, but at the present day there is hardly a conductor left who will not avail himself of the 'original' Bruckner. It is interesting to note that Wilhelm Furtwängler, one of the great Bruckner conductors, who had grown up in the tradition of the revised versions and consequently had many initial reservations about the original versions, had this to say on the subject: 'For our knowledge of Bruckner's musical language, Bruckner's stylistic will and depth of feeling, these original versions are exceedingly important and relevant. The main differences are to be found both in orchestration and in tempo relations; in both cases the original versions are characterised by greater simplicity, uniformity and directness, and they appear to correspond more closely to Bruckner's spacious concept of music. In general the many cuts which have been restored in the original versions also increase the feeling of a greater organic cohesion, not only as a detail from one bar to the next, but especially with regard to the particular work as a whole. In those cases where the cuts were made with the greatest ruthlessness—the Finale of No. 5 was reduced by 122 bars as opposed to the present version— there can be no question about the greater power, clarity and effectiveness of the original. One might almost say that this most monumental Finale of the entire musical literature of the world has been given to us anew.'

The Complete Edition was commissioned jointly by the I.B.S. and the Austrian National Library, to whom Bruckner had bequeathed his original manuscripts, and its publication was entrusted to the *Musikwissenschaftlicher Verlag*. The progress of the Complete Edition was, however, beset with many difficulties resulting from the political and historical events of 1933–45. The *Musikwissenschatlicher Verlag*, which was originally based both in Leipzig and Vienna, was completely transferred to Leipzig after the *Anschluss* of Austria in 1938, and its name was changed to *Brucknerverlag*. It is very much to be regretted that during this era the I.B.S., despite its purely cultural aims, was made the unwitting object of nationalistic propaganda which temporarily did much harm to its reputation. After the war, in 1947, the *Brucknerverlag* in Leipzig having been expropriated, it was re-established in Western Germany in Wiesbaden and subsequently transferred to Kassel. The *Musikwissenschaftlicher Verlag* began a new existence in Vienna after the war, and it has again been entrusted with the publication of the new Complete Edition.

Up to the end of the war in 1945, the following works had been issued in the Complete Edition under the general editorship of Robert Haas:

Symphony No. 1 (Linz Version), ed. Haas (1934)
Symphony No. 1 (Vienna Version), ed. Haas (1934)
Symphony No. 2, ed. Haas (1938)
Symphony No. 4 (Version II), ed. Haas (1936 and 1944)
Symphony No. 5, ed. Haas (1936)

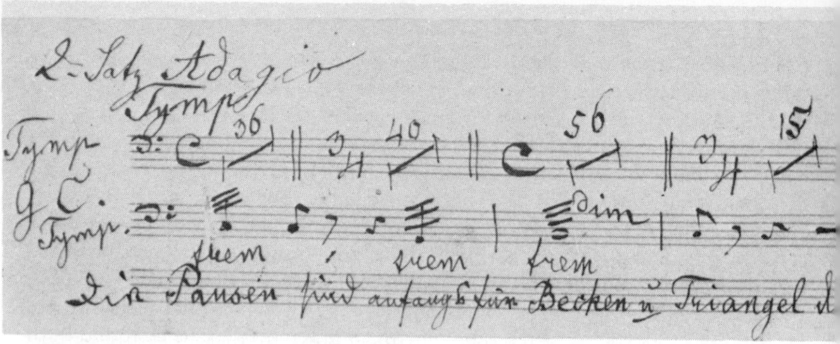

Autograph insert relating to the percussion in bars 177–182 of the Adagio, Symphony No. 7. Though opinions vary, it seems unlikely that the words 'gilt nicht' *are in Bruckner's own handwriting*

Symphony No. 6, ed. Haas (1935)
Symphony No. 7, ed. Haas (1944)
Symphony No. 8 (Version II), ed. Haas (1935)
Symphony No. 9, ed. Orel (1934)
Four Orchestral Pieces, ed. Orel (1934)
Missa Solemnis in B-flat minor, ed. Haas (1934)
Mass in E minor (Version of 1882), ed. Haas & Nowak (1940)
Mass in F minor, ed. Haas (1944)
Requiem in D minor, ed. Haas (1931)

With regard to the 4th Symphony it should be noted that this was issued twice (in 1936 and 1944), as between these two dates the engraver's copy came to light which necessitated certain minor alterations. The 1936 score of this symphony also included the second version of the Finale of 1878 (the so-called '*Volksfest*'), and together with the 9th Symphony Alfred Orel also published the sketches of the Finale as well as the two discarded Trios for the Scherzo in F and F-sharp.

In connection with the foregoing one further publication must be mentioned which, although strictly speaking it does not form part of the Complete Edition, nevertheless belongs to it in spirit:

Symphony No. 3 (Version II), ed. Oeser (1950, Brucknerverlag)

Since its resuscitation after the war, the *Musikwissenschaftlicher Verlag* has again taken up the publication of the Complete Edition. Under the editorship of Leopold Nowak most of the works which had been previously available have been re-issued since 1951, and several new works have been added. For the sake of completeness, the volumes available at the time of writing (October 1969) are listed herewith:

Vol. I/1	Symphony No. 1 (Linz Version of 1865/66), ed. Nowak (1953)
Vol. II	Symphony No. 2 (Version II of 1877), ed. Nowak (1965)

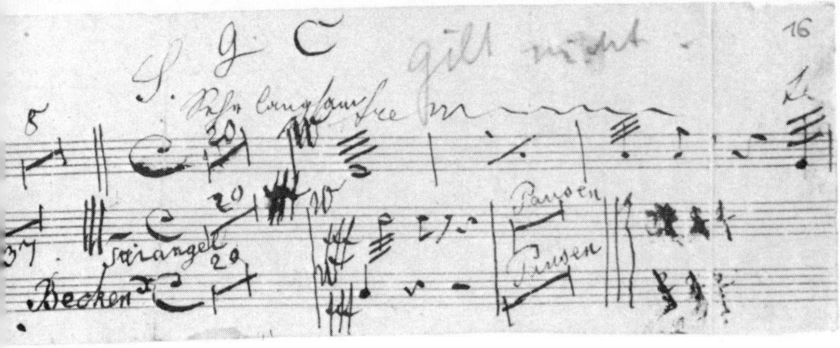

Vol III/3	Symphony No. 3 (Version of 1889), ed. Nowak (1959)
Vol. IV/2	Symphony No. 4 (Version II of 1878/80), ed. Nowak (1953)
Vol. V	Symphony No. 5, ed. Nowak (1951)
Vol. VI	Symphony No. 6, ed. Nowak (1952)
Vol. VII	Symphony No. 7, ed. Nowak (1954)
Vol. VIII/1	Symphony No. 8 (Version I of 1887) (in preparation)
Vol. VIII/2	Symphony No. 8 (Version II of 1890), ed. Nowak (1955)
Vol. IX	Symphony No. 9, ed. Nowak (1951)
Vol. XI	Symphony No. 0, ed. Nowak (1968)
Vol. XIII/1	String Quartet, ed. Nowak (1955)
Vol. XIII/2	String Quintet and Intermezzo, ed. Nowak (1963)
Vol. XIV	Requiem, ed. Nowak (1966)
Vol. XV	Missa Solemnis (in preparation)
Vol. XVI	Mass in D minor, ed. Nowak (1957)
Vol. XVII/2	Mass in E minor (Version of 1882), ed. Nowak (1959)
Vol. XVIII	Mass in F minor, ed. Nowak (1960)
Vol. XIX	Te Deum, ed. Nowak (1962)
Vol. XX/6	Psalm 150, ed. Grasberger (1964)
Vol. XXI	Shorter Sacred Works (in preparation)

As during recent years the work of Leopold Nowak has come under attack from certain quarters, at times in a most undignified and aggressive manner, a few comments on this subject would be appropriate. As can be seen from the above lists of publications, the following Bruckner works have appeared in the Complete Edition in both the Haas and the Nowak editions:

Symphony No. 1 (Linz Version)
Symphony No. 2 (Version II)
Symphony No. 4 (Version II)
Symphony No. 5
Symphony No. 6
Symphony No. 7

Last pages of the first movements of the autograph scores of Symphony No. 8. (a) First version of 1884–87 (above), (b) second version of 1889–90 (right)

Symphony No. 8 (Version II)
Symphony No. 9
Mass in E minor
Mass in F minor
Requiem

In the majority of cases (the Symphonies No. 1, No. 5, No. 6 and No. 9, the Mass in E minor and the Requiem) the 'Haas' and 'Nowak' versions are virtually identical, and the revision by Leopold Nowak in principle confined itself to the correction of printer's errors and oversights. In the case of the Symphony No. 4 and the Mass in F minor the divergences between Haas and Nowak are due to new material which has come to light (in the instance of the Symphony No. 4 a score in the possession of the Columbia University Library, New York, which hitherto had not been taken into account). In Symphony No. 7, Robert Haas had eliminated a number of dynamic and tempo markings, as these were not in Bruckner's own handwriting; Leopold Nowak, however, is of the

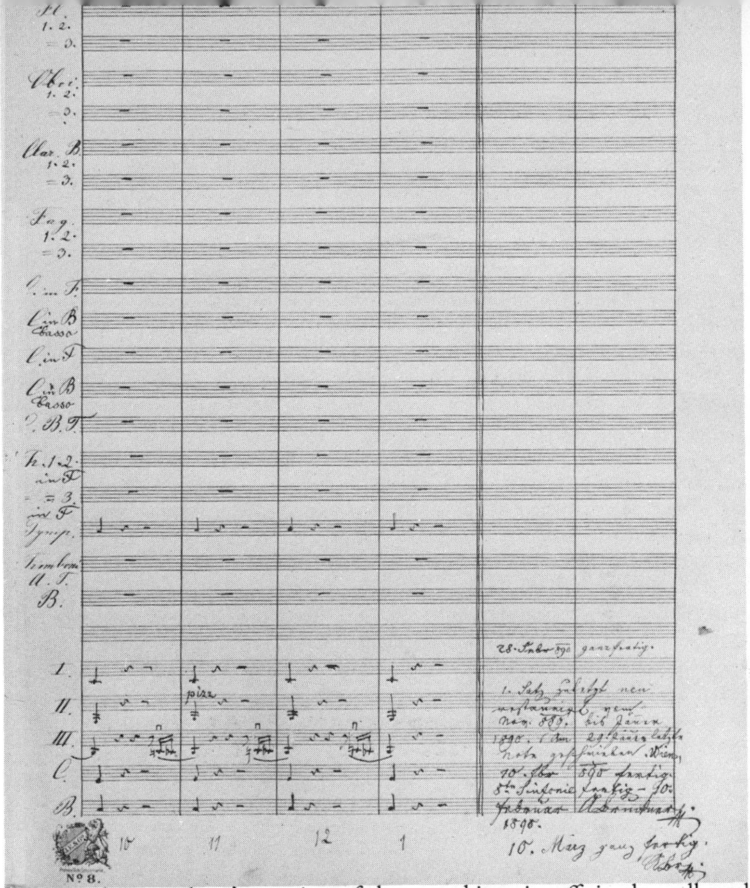

opinion that Bruckner's sanction of these markings is sufficiently well established by a number of reports and comments, and consequently he has reinstated them in his score, albeit in brackets. (Regarding the famous cymbal clash in the slow movement, cf. both the Haas and Nowak forewords to the scores of Symphony No. 7.) There remains the vexing question of the 2nd versions of Symphonies No. 2 and No. 8, and here the main problem is that of certain cuts. The great difficulty in assessing these is the following: it is perfectly clear that much of the revision work on which Bruckner was engaged throughout his life was of his own choosing, a never ending striving for perfection. On the other hand it is equally clear that certain alterations were made without his knowledge or even against his will, and these obviously found no place in the Complete Edition. But there remain a number of alterations which Bruckner made himself, though at a time when his self-confidence was at a low ebb, and when he was likely to succumb, against his better judgment possibly, to the insistent advice of his pupils and his friends. For this reason, in the case of Symphonies No. 2 and No. 8, Robert Haas has restored some material which Bruckner excised in making his second versions, inserting the corresponding passages from the respective first versions. By contrast, Leopold Nowak holds the view that, as the Complete Edition will eventually publish both the first and the second versions of these symphonies, it would be unjustifiable and misleading to include sections from one version in the other. It is of interest to read his own comment on this matter in the preface to his edition of Symphony No. 2 (Version II) (Complete Edition Vol. II): 'This of course entails the loss, particularly in the Finale, of a number of passages that one is loath to omit, and this in turn poses a series of problems that defy a universally satisfactory solution.' The crux of the matter is that there is only one person who could give the ultimate solution to the problem, and he is no longer available to be consulted: Anton Bruckner himself. It cannot be stressed too emphatically that both Robert Haas and Leopold Nowak have approached the problem with the utmost integrity and most sincere devotion to the cause of Bruckner. The difference between them is merely one of individual approach: Haas tackled the question from an artistic point of view, attempting to present the works under discussion in the purest spirit of Bruckner, and musically speaking his solutions are perhaps the more satisfying; Nowak by comparison adopts a more philologically scientific attitude, and from the musicological angle his conclusions are irreproachable and unassailable. It would be futile to pursue the matter any further in this context: in making the choice between the 'Haas' and 'Nowak' versions it is up to each and every performer to follow the dictates of his individual inclination and his artistic conscience.

Finally a chronological list of some of the first performances which took place in the original versions may be of interest:

2 April 1932	Munich:	Symphony No. 9 (under Hausegger)
4 September 1934	Aachen:	Symphony No. 1 (Linz Version)(under Raabe)
9 October 1935	Dresden:	Symphony No. 6 (under van Kempen)
20 October 1935	Munich:	Symphony No. 5 (under Hausegger)
1 March 1936	Leipzig:	Symphony No. 4 (Version II) (under Weisbach)
29 April 1938	Hamburg:	Symphony No. 2 (under E. Jochum)
5 July 1939	Hamburg:	Symphony No. 8 (Version II) (under Furtwängler)
9 April 1940	Leipzig:	Mass in E minor (Version of 1882) (under J. N. David)

Recommended Reading and Listening

Books

A vast number of books on the subject of Bruckner have been published, most of them in German, but as the majority of these bear the simple title 'Anton Bruckner' little purpose would be served in enumerating them. Instead it is proposed to mention here the most important of them, at the same time giving some indication as to the line which they pursue, in the hope that thereby interest in further reading will be stimulated.

The standard work is *Anton Bruckner* by August Göllerich, Bruckner's own appointed biographer, completed by Max Auer (4 Vol., Regensburg, 1922–36). This work, however, contains far more material than is required by any save those who wish to study Bruckner in utmost detail. The same applies to the excellent *Bruckner* by Ernst Kurth (2 Vols., Berlin, 1925) which goes into the actual music in great detail, treating it largely from the romantic and philosophical aspect. Unfortunately this excellent work is somewhat dated; at the time the original versions of many works were not yet available, so that all his analyses are based on the revised versions in which these works first appeared in print.

Of the larger scale works through which the subject is most easily approachable in detail, the best is undoubtedly *Anton Bruckner, sein Leben und Werk* by Max Auer (Vienna, 1931; 6th edition, Vienna-Munich-Zürich, 1966). It is basically a biography which, however, also incorporates much analytical information. Robert Haas' *Anton Bruckner* (Potsdam, 1934) follows along the same lines but goes into more technical detail, whereas Alfred Orel's excellent *Anton Bruckner: das Werk, der Künstler, die Zeit* (Vienna-Leipzig, 1925) concerns itself mainly with the music, dealing with the various aspects (harmony, thematic treatment, rhythm, symphonic conception, orchestration, form) in turn and consequently requires a certain amount of basic theoretical knowledge of such matters. For a concise but all-embracing survey of Bruckner

Friedrich Blume's article in *Die Musik in Geschichte und Gegenwart* (Kassel-Basel, 1952, Vol. 2, pp. 341 ff.) is highly to be recommended, also Erich Schwebsch, *Anton Bruckner* (Stuttgart, 1921). On a smaller scale *Das kleine Brucknerbuch* by Josef Lassl (Salzburg, 1965) must be mentioned especially for its excellent pictorial coverage, and perhaps one of the best of the recent publications is *Anton Bruckner, Musik und Leben* by Leopold Nowak (Vienna, 1964). Although this last book is primarily intended for younger people, it is written in a most engaging conversational style and will furnish instruction and enjoyment to old and young alike. Another worthwhile recent publication is G. F. Wehle's *Anton Bruckner im Spiegel seiner Zeitgenossen* (Garmisch-Partenkirchen, 1964) which largely collates information from various other sources and presents a picture of Bruckner under separate and well defined headings. Beyond the realm of the purely biographical, attention must be drawn to *Anton Bruckner, Versuch einer Deutung* by Max Dehnert (Leipzig, 1958) as well as to Bruckner's letters in *Gesammelte Briefe* (ed. Gräflinger & Auer, 2 Vols., Regensburg, 1924).

A very fine survey of Bruckner's symphonic work is given in *Die Symphonie Anton Bruckners* by August Halm (Munich, 1914), and *Anton Bruckner im Spiegel seiner Zeit*, edited by Norbert Tschulik (Vienna, 1965) is a little paper-bound volume which gives a very clear picture of Bruckner as seen by his contemporaries. From amongst the circle around Bruckner several books of memoirs have also been published, notably those by Eckstein (*Erinnerungen an Anton Bruckner*, Vienna, 1924), Hruby (*Meine Erinnerungen an Anton Bruckner*, Vienna, 1901) and Klose (*Meine Lehrjahre bei Bruckner*, Ratisbon, 1927), but although these furnish fascinating reading it must also be stressed that some of the information they contain is of the anecdotal character discussed earlier.

As Bruckner's music became known only very gradually in the non-German speaking countries, it is not surprising that there is a comparative dearth of Bruckner literature in languages other than German. In French the two most important works are *La Vie et l'oeuvre d'Anton Bruckner* by Armand Machabey (Paris, 1945) and Léon van Vassenhove's *Anton Bruckner* (Neuchâtel, 1942), and the book which offers the easiest approach in English is possibly *Anton Bruckner* by Erwin Doernberg (London, 1960), although it is marred by some factual errors as well as a somewhat caustic attack on Leopold Nowak. However, the second part of this book gives interesting analyses of the nine symphonies, with many music examples, and these may be of assistance to those who wish to make themselves more intimately acquainted with Bruckner's music. On the subject of the symphonies a brief but very valuable treatise is to be found in the B.B.C. Publication (1963) *Bruckner and the Symphony* by Robert Simpson, one of the foremost British Bruckner authorities, whose book *The Essence of Bruckner* has already been mentioned (see note p. 147).

Recordings

As records are being issued and deleted with increasing frequency, it is futile to attempt the compilation of a discography, as such a list is bound to be obsolete by the time this book comes before the public. It is therefore thought that a much more useful purpose will be served if individual interpreters of Bruckner's music are discussed from the point of view of their intrinsic approach. Of these, in the first instance, mention must be made of those conductors who are no longer alive, but who have established a great reputation as Bruckner interpreters and whose work is, to some extent, still available on records—though it must be stressed that, as their, recordings were all made a number of years ago, they are not up to the present-day standards as regards their technical quality. Foremost amongst this group are the recordings of *Wilhelm Furtwängler* (on H.M.V., Electrola, Deutsche Grammophon and Unicorn). Furtwängler always had a highly individual style, and this is also true of his readings of Bruckner symphonies, but there is hardly another artist who could fuse the whole of a Bruckner symphony into such a dramatic and organic entity. *Bruno Walter* (on C.B.S.) takes a much gentler and perhaps more spiritualised view, whilst *Carl Schuricht* (on H.M.V., Electrola) has a more matter-of-fact approach which is very faithful to the letter of the score. *Volkmar Andreae* (on Philips, Amadeo) must not be overlooked, for although he is not such a well known name his readings of Bruckner's music are very clean and straight forward, and his particular merit is the attention and devotion he has lavished on the earlier and lesser known symphonies. *Hans Knappertsbusch*, although he must also number amongst the great Bruckner conductors of the first half of this century, unfortunately persisted to the end in adhering to the unauthentic, revised versions.

Of the living conductors the first name that comes to mind is that of *Otto Klemperer* (on Columbia) whose performances are examples of towering strength and inner cohesion. Klemperer takes very few liberties with the score which has lead certain critics to refer to his readings as 'stodgy', but there are hardly any other recordings which make the form and structure of the works so clear and apparent. By contrast *Eugen Jochum* (on Deutsche Grammophon) allows himself infinite freedom, especially in matters of tempo, and yet his readings are in the truest spirit of Bruckner; he must certainly be regarded as one of the greatest Bruckner conductors alive. *Georg Solti* (on Decca) undoubtedly gives the most dramatic performances. His readings are laden with emotion and dynamic drive, bringing the supposed Wagnerian element very effectively to the fore. *Herbert von Karajan* (on Columbia) has for many years been represented by only one Bruckner symphony (No. 8) on record, but according to information received more Bruckner recordings under his baton are imminent and, to judge by this one example, these should be of excellent quality.

The outstanding Bruckner conductor of the younger generation is *Bernard Haitink*, whose readings of Bruckner (on Philips) are perhaps amongst the finest available as they are in the purest style, neither adding to nor subtracting from the spirit or the letter of the score, and thereby he never interposes his own subjective personality between Bruckner and the listener. Lastly mention must be made of *Istvan Kertesz* (on Decca) who, although he does not rank amongst those conductors who have made Bruckner their special field, is so far represented by one very fine recording of the 4th Symphony.

Finally the attention of all lovers of Bruckner's music must be directed to two conductors whose performances are of outstandingly high quality, but who to date have not yet committed any Bruckner interpretations to record: *Rudolf Kempe* and *Rafael Kubelik*.

Chronological List of Compositions

The following chronological list of Bruckner's completed and extant compositions is based largely on that given by Max Auer. Dates of composition refer to the completion of the first known version; dubious dates are indicated by (?). Works of which Bruckner's authorship is doubtful are placed in *italics*. The page numbers in the last column indicate those places where the most important mentions of the works occur in the main sections of the book. Where no page reference is given, these works are not discussed within the text.

Abbreviations	
cor.	horn
ma. ch.	male voice chorus
mi. ch.	mixed voice chorus
orch.	orchestra
org.	organ
pf.	pianoforte
pt.	part
quart.	quartet
S-A-T-B	solo soprano-alto-tenor-bass
tr.	trumpet
tromb.	trombone
vl.	violin

Composition	*Composed*	*Page*
'Pange lingua' in C (mi. ch.)	1835 (?)	18
4 Preludes (org.)	1836 (?)	18
Prelude in E-flat (org.)	1837 (?)	18
Mass in C (A, mi. ch., 2 cor.)	1842 (?)	25
'Tafellied' (ma. ch.)	1843	28
'Libera' in F (mi. ch. and org.)	1843 (?)	28
'Tantum ergo' in D	1843	28
Chorale Mass for Maundy Thursday (mi. ch. (includes 'Christus factus est' I)	1844	28
Cantata 'Vergissmeinnicht' (S-A-T-B, mi. ch. and pf.)	1845	28
'Herz-Jesu-Lied' (mi. ch. and org.)	1845 (?)	
'O du liebes Jesukind' (voice and org.)	1845 (?)	
'Das Lied vom deutschen Vaterland' (ma. ch.)	1845 (?)	
2 'Asperges me' (mi. ch. and org.)	1845 (?)	
'Ständchen' (ma. ch.)	1846 (?)	

Composition	Composed	Page
5 'Tantum ergo' in E-flat, C, B-flat, A-flat and D (mi. ch., No. 5 with org.)	1846	
2 Pieces in D minor (org.)	1846 (?)	
'Festlied' (ma. ch.)	1846 (?)	
Prelude and Fugue in C minor (org.)	1847	
Chorale 'Dir, Herr, Dir will ich mich ergeben' (mi. ch.)	1847 (?)	
'Der Lehrerstand' (ma. ch.)	1847 (?)	
Aequale (3 tromb.)	1847	
Chorale 'In jener letzten der Nächte' in F minor	1848	
'Sternschnuppen' (ma. ch.)	1848 (?)	
'Tantum ergo' in A (mi. ch. and org.)	1848 (?)	
Requiem in D minor (S-A-T-B, mi. ch., orch. and org.)	1849	31, 141
Lancier-Quadrille (pf.)	1850 (?)	
Steiermärker (pf.)	1850 (?)	
'Frühlingslied' (voice and pf.)	1851	
2 'Motti' (ma. ch.)	1851	
'Das edle Herz' (ma. ch.)	1851 (?)	
Cantata 'Entsagen' (soli, mi. ch. and org.)	1851 (?)	
2 'Totenlieder' in F and D (mi. ch.)	1852	
'Die Geburt' (ma. ch.)	1852	
Magnificat in B-flat (S-A-T-B, mi. ch. and orch.)	1852	
Cantata 'Auf, Brüder, auf zur frohen Feier' (solo quart. and brass)	1852	
Psalm 114 (5-pt. mi. ch. and 3 tromb.)	1852	32
Psalm 22 (mi. ch. and pf.)	1852	
3 Pieces (pf. duet)	1852–54	
'Tantum ergo' in B-flat (mi. ch., 2 vl., 2 tr. and org.)	1854 (?)	
'Vor Arneths Grab' (ma. ch.)	1854	32
'Libera' in F minor (mi. ch.)	1854	32
Missa solemnis in B-flat minor (S-A-T-B, mi. ch. and orch.)	1854	32, 142
Quadrille (pf. duet)	1854 (?)	
Cantata 'Auf, Brüder, auf, die Saiten zur Hand' (soli, mi. ch. and orch.)	1855	
'St. Jodok spross aus edlem Stamm' (soli, mi. ch. and pf.)	1855	
'Des Dankes Wort sei mir gegönnt' (T-B, ma. ch.)	1855	
Piece in E-flat (pf.)	1856 (?)	
'Ave Maria' in F (mi. ch. and org.)	1856	38
'Amaranths Waldeslieder' (voice and pf.)	1858 (?)	
Psalm 146 (soli, mi. ch. and orch.)	1860 (?)	38
'Am Grabe' (ma. ch.)	1861	38
'Ave Maria' (7-pt. mi. ch.)	1861	38
'Afferentur' (mi. ch., 3 tromb. and org.)	1861	42
Fugue in D minor (org.)	1861	42
'Du bist wie eine Blume' (S-A-T-B)	1862	
'Das edle Herz' (mi. ch.)	1862 (?)	
'Der Abendhimmel' (T-T-B-B)	1862 (?)	
Festive Cantata 'Preiset den Herrn' (soli, mi. ch. and wind band)	1862	
'*Apollomarsch*' (military band)	1862 (?)	43
String Quartet in C minor	1862	43, 146
March in D minor (orch.)	1862	43
3 Orchestral pieces in E-flat, E minor and F (orch.)	1862	43
Overture in G minor (orch.)	1863	45
Symphony in F minor (orch.)	1863	45, 146
Psalm 112 (mi. ch. and orch.)	1863	45

Composition	*Composed*	*Page*
'Germanenzug' (ma. ch. and brass band)	1863	45
'Stille Betchratung an einem Herbstabend' (pf.)	1863	
Symphony No. 0 in D minor (orch.)	1864	45, 146
'Um Mitternacht' I (A, ma. ch. and pf.)	1864	
'Herbstlied' (S-S, ma. ch. and pf.)	1864	
Mass No. 1 in D minor (S-A-T-B, mi. ch. and orch.)	1864	45, 142
'Trauungslied' (ma. ch. and org.)	1865	
March in E-flat (military band)	1865	
'Abendklänge' (vl. and pf.)	1866	47
'Der Abendhimmel' (ma. ch.)	1866	47
'O könnt' ich dich beglücken' (soli, ma. ch.)	1866	47
'Vaterländisches Weinlied' (ma. ch.)	1866	47
Symphony No. 1 in C minor (orch.)	1866	46, 48, 170
Mass No. 2 in E minor (8-pt. mi. ch. and wind band)	1866	47, 142, 144
Mass No. 3 in F minor (S-A-T-B, mi. ch., orch. and org.)	1868	48, 60, 142
'Inveni David' (ma. ch. and 4 tromb.)	1868	
Fantasie in E-flat (pf.)	1868	
'Motto' (mi. ch.)	1868	
'Pange lingua' (phrygian) (mi. ch.)	1868	
Hymnus St. Angeli custodem 'Iam lucis' (mi. ch.)	1868	
'Asperges me' in F (mi. ch.)	1868 (?)	
'Erinnerung' (pf.)	1868 (?)	
'Im April' (voice and pf.)	1868 (?)	
'Mein Herz und deine Stimme' (voice and pf.)	1868 (?)	
'Herbstkummer' (voice and pf.)	1868 (?)	
'Motto für die Liedertafel Sierning'	1868 (?)	
'Locus iste' (mi. ch.)	1869	52
'Mitternacht' (T, ma. ch. and pf.)	1870	52
Symphony No. 2 in C minor (orch.)	1872	58, 61, 170
Symphony No. 3 in D minor (orch.)	1873	61, 72, 74, 93, 171
Symphony No. 4 in E-flat (orch.)	1874	67, 72, 78, 171
'Das hohe Lied' (soli, ma. ch. and wind band)	1876	
Symphony No. 5 in B-flat (orch.)	1877	67, 153ff, 171
'Trösterin Musik' (ma. ch. and org.)	1877	
'Abendzauber' (ma. ch. and 4 cor.)	1878	
'Tota pulchra es' (T, mi. ch. and org.)	1878	74
'Zwei Herzen haben sich gefunden' (ma. ch.)	1878	
String Quintet in F	1879	74, 75, 146
'Christus factus est' II (6-pt. mi. ch., 3 tromb. and strings)	1879	75
Intermezzo for String Quintet	1879	75
'Os justi' (mi. ch.)	1879	75
Symphony No. 6 in A (orch.)	1881	75, 78, 171
'Sängerbund' (ma. ch.)	1882	
'Ave Maria' (A and org.)	1882	79
Symphony No. 7 in E (orch.)	1883	79, 80, 81, 83, 171

Composition	*Composed*	*Page*
Te Deum (S-A-T-B, mi. ch., orch. and org.)	1884	80, 81, 96, 141
'Christus factus est' III (7 pt. mi. ch.)	1884	81
'Salvum fac' (mi. ch.)	1884	81
Prelude in C (harmonium)	1884	81
'Ecce sacerdos' (mi. ch., 3 tromb. and org.)	1885	81
'Virga Jesse' (mi. ch.)	1885	86
'Um Mitternacht' II (T, ma. ch.)	1886	86
Symphony No. 8 in C minor (orch.)	1887	89, 93, 94, 172
'Träumen und Wachen' (T, ma. ch.)	1890	95
'Vexilla regis' (mi. ch.)	1892	99
'Das deutsche Lied' (ma. ch. and brass band)	1892	99
Psalm 150 (S, mi. ch., orch. and org.)	1892	99, 141
'Helgoland' (ma. ch. and orch.)	1893	99
Symphony No. 9 in D minor (orch.) (unfinished at his death)		106, 108, 155, 172

Illustrations

Acknowledgements

The author wishes to express his gratitude to the following institutions and persons who have so kindly given their assistance in the preparation of this book: Anglo-Austrian Society, London, Austrian Institute, London, Austrian National Library (Music Department), Vienna, Gesellschaft der Musikfreunde, Vienna, Musikwissenschaftlicher Verlag, Vienna; Bärenreiter Musicaphon, Cantate Records, Decca Record Co., Deutsche Grammophon-Gesellschaft, Electrola GmbH., E.M.I. Records, Philips Records, Saga Records, Vox Productions; Julius Bayer, Deryck Cooke, Franz S. Forster, Prof. Rudolf Gamsjäger, Ing. Josef Hack, Fam. J. Hagler, Dir. Johann Krichbaum, Fr. Augustinus Franz Kropfreiter, Frau Dr. Mitringer, Hofrat Univ. Prof. Dr. Leopold Nowak, Dr. Fritz Oeser, Mr. and Mrs. A. R. N. Ratcliff, Dr. Robert Simpson, Frau K. Smetana-Furegg, Prof. Dr. Hugo Zelzer.

Grateful acknowledgements are also due to the late Prof. Dr. Max Auer, whose writings furnished so much valuable information.

Index of Persons and Places